D1200595

INTRODUCING
ISSUES WITH
OPPOSING
VIEWPOINTS®

Pollution

Other books in the Introducing Issues
with Opposing Viewpoints series:

INTRODUCING
ISSUES WITH
OPPOSING
VIEWPOINTS®

Pollution

Cynthia A. Bily, *Book Editor*

Christine Nasso, *Publisher*
Elizabeth Des Chenes, *Managing Editor*

GREENHAVEN PRESS

An imprint of Thomson Gale, a part of The Thomson Corporation

THOMSON
™
GALE

Detroit • New York • San Francisco • San Diego • New Haven, Conn. • Waterville, Maine • London • Munich

For more information, contact
Greenhaven Press
27500 Drake Rd.
Farmington Hills, MI 48331-3535
Or you can visit our Internet site at http://www.gale.com

Articles in Greenhaven Press anthologies are often edited for length to meet page requirements. In addition, original titles of these works are changed to clearly present the main thesis and to explicitly indicate the author's opinion. Every effort is made to ensure that Greenhaven Press accurately reflects the original intent of the authors.

Every effort has been made to trace the owners of copyrighted material.

LIBRARY OF CONGRESS CATALOGING-IN-PUBLICATION DATA

Pollution / Cynthia A. Bily, book editor.
    p. cm. — (Introducing issues with opposing viewpoints)
  Includes bibliographical references and index.
ISBN 0-7377-3546-5 (hardcover : alk. paper)
    1. Pollution—Juvenile literature. 2. Environmental protection—Juvenile literature.
I. Bily, Cynthia A.
  TD176.P653 2006
  363.73—dc22
                                         2006021462

Printed in the United States of America

Contents

Foreword

Indulging in a wide spectrum of ideas, beliefs, and perspectives is a critical cornerstone of democracy. After all, it is often debates over differences of opinion, such as whether to legalize abortion, how to treat prisoners, or when to enact the death penalty, that shape our society and drive it forward. Such diversity of thought is frequently regarded as the hallmark of a healthy and civilized culture. As the Reverend Clifford Schutjer of the First Congregational Church in Mansfield, Ohio, declared in a 2001 sermon, "Surrounding oneself with only like-minded people, restricting what we listen to or read only to what we find agreeable is irresponsible. Refusing to entertain doubts once we make up our minds is a subtle but deadly form of arrogance." With this advice in mind, Introducing Issues with Opposing Viewpoints books aim to open readers' minds to the critically divergent views that comprise our world's most important debates.

Introducing Issues with Opposing Viewpoints simplifies for students the enormous and often overwhelming mass of material now available via print and electronic media. Collected in every volume is an array of opinions that captures the essence of a particular controversy or topic. Introducing Issues with Opposing Viewpoints books embody the spirit of nineteenth-century journalist Charles A. Dana's axiom: "Fight for your opinions, but do not believe that they contain the whole truth, or the only truth." Absorbing such contrasting opinions teaches students to analyze the strength of an argument and compare it to its opposition. From this process readers can inform and strengthen their own opinions, or be exposed to new information that will change their minds. Introducing Issues with Opposing Viewpoints is a mosaic of different voices. The authors are statesmen, pundits, academics, journalists, corporations, and ordinary people who have felt compelled to share their experiences and ideas in a public forum. Their words have been collected from newspapers, journals, books, speeches, interviews, and the Internet, the fastest growing body of opinionated material in the world.

Introducing Issues with Opposing Viewpoints shares many of the well-known features of its critically acclaimed parent series, Opposing Viewpoints. The articles are presented in a pro/con format, allowing readers to absorb divergent perspectives side by side. Active reading questions preface each viewpoint, requiring the student to approach the material thoughtfully and carefully. Useful charts, graphs, and cartoons supplement each article. A thorough introduction provides readers with crucial background on an issue. An annotated bibliography points the reader toward articles, books, and Web sites that contain additional information on the topic. An appendix of organizations to contact contains a wide variety of charities, nonprofit organizations, political groups, and private enterprises that each hold a position on the issue at hand. Finally, a comprehensive index allows readers to locate content quickly and efficiently.

Introducing Issues with Opposing Viewpoints is also significantly different from Opposing Viewpoints. As the series title implies, its presentation will help introduce students to the concept of opposing viewpoints, and learn to use this material to aid in critical writing and debate. The series' four-color, accessible format makes the books attractive and inviting to readers of all levels. In addition, each viewpoint has been carefully edited to maximize a reader's understanding of the content. Short but thorough viewpoints capture the essence of an argument. A substantial, thought-provoking essay question placed at the end of each viewpoint asks the student to further investigate the issues raised in the viewpoint, compare and contrast two authors' arguments, or consider how one might go about forming an opinion on the topic at hand. Each viewpoint contains sidebars that include at-a-glance information and handy statistics. A Facts About section located in the back of the book further supplies students with relevant facts and figures.

Following in the tradition of the Opposing Viewpoints series, Greenhaven Press continues to provide readers with invaluable exposure to the controversial issues that shape our world. As John Stuart Mill once wrote: "The only way in which a human being can make some approach to knowing the whole of a subject is by hearing what can be said about it by persons of every variety of opinion and studying all modes in which it can be looked at by every character of mind. No wise man ever acquired his wisdom in any mode but this." It is to this principle that Introducing Issues with Opposing Viewpoints books are dedicated.

Introduction

"In the past three decades, environmental measures have cleared up much of the visible pollution that once hovered menacingly over urban areas, but smog, soot and haze persist. . . . Further, we've learned that air pollution can be deadly even if we can't see it."

—Natural Resources Defense Council, 2006

Pollution in the twenty-first century is a complicated issue because it is often an invisible issue. In the United States, most people have access to fresh-tasting, crystal-clear water and to air that looks clean and is odorless. With the exception of a school poster project or a toxic waste collection on Earth Day, most go about their daily lives without giving pollution a thought. For environmentalists, this indifference is both a reason for celebration and a cause for concern. The fact that the most obvious forms of pollution have been cleaned up is good news. But the remaining forms of pollution will be harder to address because they are harder to see.

It has not always been this way. In the 1960s and 1970s pollution was so dramatic that it could not be ignored. Sometimes-sensational cases of environmental hazards dominated the headlines, as in 1969 when the Cuyahoga River in Ohio became so polluted that the river itself caught fire and burned. In the late 1970s residents of Love Canal in New York had to be evacuated from their homes when it was revealed that highly toxic industrial waste buried in the soil was directly linked to their serious health problems. The term *smog* was coined in the 1970s to describe the visible combination of smoke and fog that settled over Los Angeles and other cities. These events led to passage of the Clean Air Act in 1970, the Clean Water Act in 1972, and other laws.

These laws forced and prompted many visible improvements. According to the U.S. House of Representatives Committee on Resources, "Environmental trendlines continue in the right direction, with cleaner air and fresh water for all Americans." Yet this does not

At a 1978 demonstration, young residents protest toxic waste buried in their neighborhood in Love Canal, New York.

mean that pollution is no longer a problem. As President George W. Bush said in 2003, "Over the past three decades we've reduced the nation's air pollution by half. But there is more to do."

When pollution is invisible, however, most citizens today cannot understand how it might still affect them. Scientific research reveals the effects: For example, fine-particle air pollution accounts for many respiratory illnesses every year. These inhaled fine particles lodge and accumulate deep within the lungs, where they may remain undetected for years until they cause symptoms.

Rivers no longer catch fire, and life has returned to Lake Erie, once declared "dead" and mourned in children's writer Dr. Seuss's 1971 book *The Lorax*. But today scientists worry about mercury pollution in water, which is by some reports dangerous even in concentrations so low that it cannot be seen or tasted by consumers.

Some pollution today is "invisible" simply because it is concentrated in sparsely inhabited or localized areas. The visible form of air pollution called haze is one example. Conservation advocate Tom Kiernan points out that "some of the worst air in the country [is] in national parks"—far away from most people's view. One reminder came in August 2005, when Hurricane Katrina drew attention to high levels of pollution on the Gulf Coast. For decades before the storm, the mouth of the Mississippi River had been a repository for industrial and agricultural chemicals washed down from the central United

The Los Angeles skyline is barely visible beneath a veil of smog.

States. Oil refineries and heavy industries had polluted the air, water, and soil, earning the region just upriver from New Orleans the nickname "Cancer Alley." But with the exception of people in the Gulf States, not many knew that the area was seriously polluted, and few people outside the immediate area are thinking about it today. Like many polluted areas, Louisiana's "Cancer Alley" is largely invisible to the rest of the nation because it is a relatively isolated area and because its residents—mostly poor and black—do not have a unified public voice or political influence.

Other kinds of pollution are similarly out of sight and out of mind. America's throwaway culture discards millions of computers, cell phones, and other electronic devices every year. Once these devices have been hauled away to landfills or shipped overseas to be recycled,

Discarded computers and other electronic equipment create an unsightly and growing problem in landfills.

it is unknown whether their components' toxic heavy metals are safely contained or properly handled. And although billions of people in other parts of the world do not have access to the relatively clean air and water that most Americans enjoy, U.S. citizens tend to think of faraway pollution as someone else's problem.

All of this means that battling pollution involves different if not more difficult challenges in the twenty-first century. Few people in the 1970s would have questioned whether pollution was a serious problem, but today basic questions about pollution are again open to debate: Is pollution getting better or getting worse? Does pollution affect people's health? Is there anything we can do about pollution? These questions are addressed by the authors of the following viewpoints.

Chapter 1

Is Pollution a Serious Problem?

Dead fish and smog show that air and water pollution are still problems in China.

Air Pollution Is a Serious Problem

> "*The results are clear: ozone is dangerous at levels currently experienced in the United States.*"

American Lung Association

The authors of the following viewpoint, excerpted from the American Lung Association's annual *State of the Air* report, argue that air pollution in the United States is a serious and worsening problem. The authors describe the two most common and most dangerous types of pollution found in the United States: particle and ozone pollution. Both kinds of pollution, the Lung Association contends, are caused in part by vehicle exhaust fumes, and both kinds present serious health risks, including disease and death.

The American Lung Association works to prevent lung disease and promote lung health.

AS YOU READ, CONSIDER THE FOLLOWING QUESTIONS:
1. According to the authors, approximately how many Americans live in areas with dangerous levels of particle pollution?
2. How do coughing and sneezing help our bodies fight off some kinds of pollution, as explained in the viewpoint?
3. What common products mentioned in the viewpoint produce some of the volatile compounds that can become raw ingredients for ozone?

American Lung Association, "Health Effects of Ozone and Particle Pollution," *State of the Air 2005,* Spring 2005, pp. 53–55, 57–58. Reproduced by permission.

Everyone's had this experience: You're sitting in traffic or driving down a highway behind a large truck with fumes spewing from the tailpipe. You wonder just what that exhaust is doing to you. Scientists have been asking the same question for some time now. What we're learning is that those fumes are made up of many complicated ingredients that can do more damage than you might think.

Not only can that black plume of smoke from the tailpipe or the graying haze settling over the city make you cough and blink, but it can do much worse—it could help take months to years off of your life. The evidence accumulates as each month new research studies pour in. Analyses undertaken over the past five years tie air pollution to shorter lives, heart disease, lung cancer, asthma attacks and serious interference with the growth and work of the lungs. . . .

Particle Pollution
The dirty, smoky part of that stream of exhaust is made of particle pollution. Twenty-six percent of the nation—76.5 million people—

A Chinese cyclist covers his mouth and nose, trying not to breathe in pollution from heavy Beijing traffic.

Dave Coverly. Reproduced by permission.

live where the air they breathe has so much particle pollution for so much of the time that their health can be at risk. But what is particle pollution? What can particles do to your health? Who is most vulnerable? And what can we do about it?

Particle pollution refers to a combination of fine solids and aerosols that are suspended in the air we breathe. But nothing about particle pollution is simple. First of all, the particles themselves are different sizes. Some are one-tenth the diameter of a strand of hair. Many are even tinier; some are so small they can only be seen with an electron microscope. Because of their size, you can't see the individual particles. You can only see the haze that forms when millions of particles

A young woman uses an inhaler to help relieve her asthma, a condition that is worsened by air pollutants.

blur the spread of sunlight in an area. You may not be able to tell when you're breathing particle pollution. And yet it is so dangerous it can take years off your life.

Particle pollution ranges in size from the tiny to the microscopic. The differences in size make a big difference in how they affect us. Our body's natural defenses help us to cough or sneeze larger particles out of our bodies. But those defenses don't keep out smaller particles, those that are smaller than 10 microns, or micrometers, in diameter, or about one-seventh the diameter of a single human hair. These smaller particles get trapped in the lungs, while the smallest are so minute they can pass through the lungs into the bloodstream, just like the essential oxygen molecules. . . .

What Can Particles Do to Your Health?

That dark smoke coming out of the truck's tailpipe is probably directly emitting carbon particles and the raw ingredients for other fine particles into the air. That dark stream mixes with exhausts from other cars, trucks and heavy equipment, as well as the exhaust plumes from power plants, factories and many other sources to create the particle pollution problem we have in many places in the U.S. today.

In the early 1990s, dozens of short-term community health studies from cities throughout the United States and around the world indicated that short-term increases in particle pollution were associated with adverse health effects ranging from increased respiratory symptoms to increased hospitalization and emergency room visits, to increased mortality from respiratory and cardiovascular disease. . . .

Particle pollution causes a broad range of health problems. Exposure worsens asthma and causes wheezing, coughing and respiratory irritation in anyone with sensitive airways. It also triggers heart attacks, cardiac arrhythmias (irregular heartbeat) and premature death.

Because of its very small size, particle pollution gets right through the nasal passage, past the trachea and deep into the lungs. The smallest of the particles can even enter the bloodstream via the lungs. . . .

Ozone Pollution

Remember that truck exhaust? As you stare at that dark and gritty smoke, be aware that you can't see all of its dangers. The dirty cloud of that truck's exhaust is a mass of particles, but hidden in the plume are the raw ingredients for the most widespread air pollutant: ozone, commonly known as smog. In two large studies this year [2005], we learned new information about ozone that confirmed for the first time the deadly effects of this old public health nemesis. . . .

> **FAST FACT**
>
> On fifty-two days in 2004, the air in California's Sequoia and Kings Canyon National Parks had enough ozone to exceed the Environmental Protection Agency's "unhealthy air" standard. Signs warned visitors against taking long hikes.

What you see coming out of the tailpipe on that truck isn't ozone, but the raw ingredients for ozone. Like some types of particle pollution, ozone is formed by chemical reactions in the atmosphere from those key raw ingredients that do come out of tailpipes, smokestacks and many other places. These essential raw ingredients for ozone, nitrogen oxides (NO_X) and hydrocarbons, or volatile organic compounds

(VOCs), are produced primarily when fossil fuels like gasoline or coal are burned or when fossil fuel–based chemicals, like paints, evaporate. When they come in contact with both heat and sunlight, these molecules combine and form ozone. NO_x is emitted from power plants, motor vehicles and other sources of high-heat combustion. VOCs are emitted from motor vehicles, chemical plants, refineries, factories, gas stations, paint and other sources. . . .

How Ozone Pollution Affects Your Health

The effects of ozone on lung health have been studied at length using laboratory animals, clinical subjects and human populations. The results are clear: ozone is dangerous at levels currently experienced in the United States. What we are still learning is just how dangerous ozone can be.

Two important studies released in late 2004 confirm that short-term exposure to ozone can kill. One study looked at 95 cities across the United States over a 14-year period. That study compared the impact of ozone on death patterns during several days after the ozone measurements. Even on days when ozone levels were below the current national standard, the researchers found an increased risk of premature death associated with increased levels of ozone. They estimated that over 3,700 deaths annually could be attributed to a 10 parts per billion increase in ozone levels. Another study, published the same week, looked at 23 European cities and found similar effects on mortality from ozone exposure.

EVALUATING THE AUTHORS' ARGUMENTS:

The viewpoint you have just read presents facts and statistics that are described using words such as "dangerous" and "deadly." How do these words affect the way you understand the viewpoint? Would the facts about particle and ozone pollution seem threatening by themselves? Explain your answer.

Air Pollution Is Not a Serious Problem

Michael Fumento

> "Since 1970, the total national emissions of the six principal pollutants . . . have been cut 48 percent."

In the following viewpoint Michael Fumento argues that the air in the United States has been getting cleaner over the past decades. Fumento concludes that stricter regulations on power plant emissions to further reduce air pollution would be expensive and would not improve Americans' health—in fact, they could lead to more deaths.

Fumento is a senior fellow at the Hudson Institute (a public policy research organization) and a nationally syndicated columnist.

AS YOU READ, CONSIDER THE FOLLOWING QUESTIONS:

1. According to the viewpoint, what is PM2.5?
2. According to Fumento, what variables did the Harvard Six Cities Study fail to consider?
3. In Fumento's view, what was the reason for many of the deaths in the French heat wave of 2003?

Michael Fumento, "Cleaner Air Brings Dirtier Tricks," *Tech Central Station,* July 9, 2004. Reproduced by permission.

How strange! The cleaner our air gets, the sicker we become. At this rate, when the air becomes absolutely pure over L.A. [Los Angeles] we'll all keel right over. Or so you might believe from a downloadable new report of a group called Clear the Air, "Dirty Power, Dirty Air."

The prettily-decorated document attempts to persuade readers to support one of two Democratic bills introduced in the Senate over a Republican one, although all three would "tighten the lid" on allowable air emissions from power plants. Not incidentally it chooses the legislation that is by far the most expensive. By its own reckoning, in the year 2020 it will cost $34 billion versus $9.3 for the alternative Democratic bill and $6.2 for what it labels the "Bush bill."

You may not think you're coughing and gasping for air, but trust them—you are. In fact, "fine particle pollution from U.S. power plants cuts short the lives of nearly 24,000 people each year, including 2,800 from lung cancer," says the report.

And we're not talking about losing a few days, but rather an average of 14 years. Air pollution also causes over 38,000 non-fatal heart attacks and more than half a million cases of asthma, we're told.

Statistics Point to Cleaner Air

Gad! Better, it seems, to smoke four packs a day of Camels than live near a coal- or oil-fired plant. (And don't even think about proposing the use of safe and clean nuclear energy; Clear the Air has never heard of it.) But if we let just a little ray of sunshine come through that soot-blackened air, here's what we find:

- Since 1970, the total national emissions of the six principal pollutants the EPA [Environmental Protection Agency] tracks have been cut 48 percent, even as energy consumption increased 42 percent and the population increased 38 percent.
- Fine particle emissions, technically known as PM2.5 (because it refers to particulate matter 2.5 micrometers or smaller in size, about 1/30 the width of a human hair), have only been tracked since 1993, but by 2002 had fallen 17 percent. In terms of air quality, they have only been measured since 1998 but by 2003 had dropped eight percent.

This is bad news?

Faulty Studies

We know that Clear the Air is playing pollution prevarication with asthma because even as dirty air levels plummeted, asthma incidence from 1980 to 1999 INCREASED by 83 percent according to the Centers for Disease Control and Prevention. . . .

A 1993 analysis, partly funded by the EPA, was called The Harvard Six Cities Study because it compared PM2.5 levels and deaths among six municipalities. As it happens, four were of no use to the researchers; so it should have been called "The Two Cities Study." Of those two, one had significantly higher PM2.5 levels and higher death rates. Aha! 'Twas fine particles that did the evil deed.

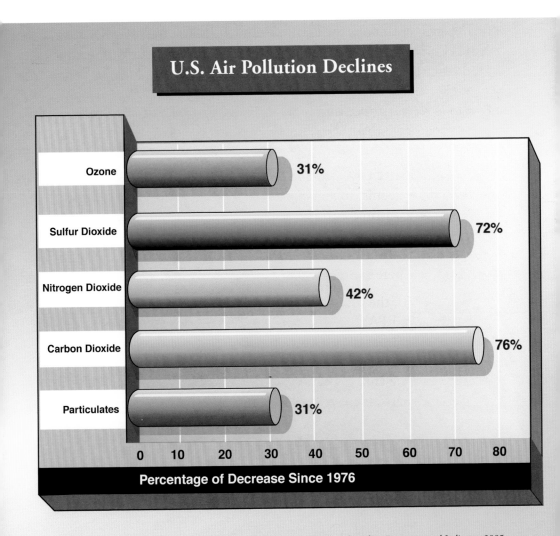

U.S. Air Pollution Declines

Ozone — 31%
Sulfur Dioxide — 72%
Nitrogen Dioxide — 42%
Carbon Dioxide — 76%
Particulates — 31%

Percentage of Decrease Since 1976

Source: Pacific Research Institute and American Enterprise Institute, *Index of Leading Environmental Indicators 2005*, www.pacificresearch.org, April 2005.

Yet among nonsmokers there was no statistically significant difference in deaths. Different smoking rates could have accounted for everything. Likewise, there was no significant difference in deaths if you excluded persons with occupational exposures to "gases, fumes, or dust."

The Role of Poverty

The researchers also didn't control for humidity or temperature and they didn't even consider income differences.

Such factors could throw off the whole study. For example the city with more deaths, Steubenville, Ohio, was considerably poorer than the comparison city of Portage, Wisconsin. "Poor persons tend to die more quickly during extreme weather conditions than wealthier ones," Roger McClellan, President Emeritus of the CIIT [Chemical Industry Institute of Toxicology] Centers for Health Research in Research Triangle Park, North Carolina, told me. As the National Institute for Environmental Health Sciences states: "The affluent citizens of this Nation enjoy better

Poor families living in poorly constructed houses like this one are more vulnerable to pollutants and extreme weather.

health than do its minority and poorer citizens. The most striking health disparities involve shorter life expectancy among the poor, as well as higher rates of cancer, birth defects, infant mortality, asthma, diabetes, and cardiovascular disease."

All the Harvard researchers necessarily showed was that poverty, not particulates, is linked to illness.

In general, the Six Cities Study was a brilliant exercise in omission of "non-useful" information. The particulate hunters carefully excised from their data any personal habit, any occupational exposure, and anything else that would result in anything other than their pre-determined conclusion. They then steadfastly refused to make public their data—even to the EPA! They admitted they didn't want others to analyze them.

FAST FACT

Between 1992 and 2003 the nation's top ten cities reduced their air pollution by 54 percent, according to the Environmental Protection Agency.

[Former EPA administrator] Carol Browner's EPA, essentially a taxpayer-supported environmentalist group, quickly grabbed onto the conclusion of the Six Cities Study, along with that of an equally skewed one from 1995 that had three of the same authors. It demanded fine particle regulation and it got it. Yet a subsequent review of all particulate studies, conducted by Fred Hutchinson Cancer Research Center epidemiologist Suresh Moolgavkar and a colleague, found no evidence that anybody has ever died from PM2.5 or larger particles. . . .

Raising Prices Could Lead to Real Deaths

On the other hand, stricter emissions regulations [as some groups have called for] clearly increase consumer energy prices and Clear the Air is hawking those which by its own admission are by far the most expensive. If my utility bill increases, I'll grumble but I can afford it. You probably can, too. It's the poor who will suffer, especially the elderly ones. They are most likely to turn off air conditioners during heat waves when the bills are the highest and their bodies can least adjust to the heat.

Last August [2003] in France, a mind-boggling 15,000 people died during a single heat wave. By the standards of much of the U.S.,

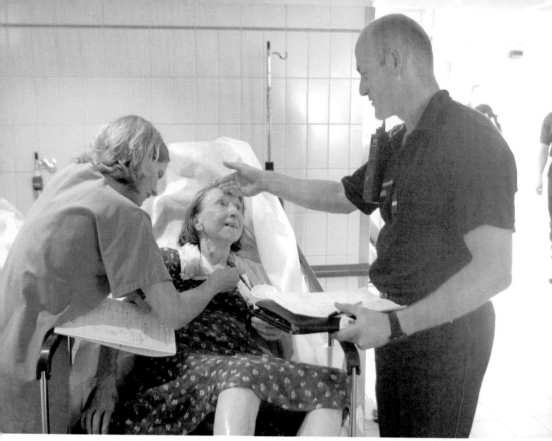

Medics attend to an elderly woman suffering from the French heat wave of 2003.

temperatures weren't that high. But air conditioning is rare in France even in hospitals and nursing homes. Why? Because taxes pushed by the French equivalents of Clear the Air drove up energy costs.

If Clear the Air gets its way, we'll be trading theoretical deaths derived through the use of smoke and mirrors for real deaths with real bodies. But until we get rid of that last piece of soot, apparently that's just the price they're willing to have us pay.

EVALUATING THE AUTHOR'S ARGUMENTS:

Michael Fumento begins his viewpoint using a sarcastic tone, poking fun at the people who disagree with him. How does this tone affect the way you respond to his ideas? Explain your answer.

Water Pollution Is a Serious Problem

Rebecca R. Wodder

"As many as 3.5 million Americans get sick each year after swimming, boating, fishing, or otherwise touching water they thought was safe."

In the following viewpoint Rebecca R. Wodder contends that water pollution from overflowing sewer systems is a widespread problem that is responsible for serious health issues. She argues that America's sewer systems are too old to handle current levels of waste. As pipes age, and as new developments push more storm water into overburdened sewer systems, pollution flows into the nation's lakes and rivers. Wodder calls for more money to be spent on upgrading sewer systems and cleanup projects.

Wodder has been president of American Rivers, a national conservation organization, since 1995. Previously she worked with another conservation group, the Wilderness Society.

AS YOU READ, CONSIDER THE FOLLOWING QUESTIONS:

1. According to the viewpoint, how many gallons of sewage escape from American sewer systems each year?
2. When did Congress pass the Clean Water Act, as stated in the viewpoint?
3. Name four infectious diseases found in untreated sewage.

Where does human waste mingle with household chemicals, personal hygiene products, pharmaceuticals, and everything else that goes down the drains in American homes and businesses? In sewers.

And what can you get when rain, pesticides, fertilizers, automotive chemicals, and trash run off the streets and down the gutters into those very same sewers? Sewage backing up into people's basements. Sewage spilling onto streets and parks. Sewage pouring into rivers and streams.

Each year, more than 860 billion gallons of this vile brew escapes sewer systems across the country. That's enough to flood all of Pennsylvania ankle-deep. It's enough for every American to take one bath each week for an entire year.

After bursting out of a pipe or manhole cover, this foul slurry pollutes the nearest body of water. Downstream, some of it may be pumped out, treated, and piped into more homes and businesses. From there, it goes back into a sewer system, and the cycle resumes.

This is the situation along the Susquehanna River—which tops [2005's] America's Most Endangered Rivers list. One hundred and twenty three major sewer systems in the Susquehanna River watershed link toilets and faucets from New York to Maryland. Where the Susquehanna widens and becomes the Chesapeake Bay, vanishing sea grasses and dwindling seafood harvests provide evidence of poor sewage treatment and frequent sewage spills upstream.

A Threat to Human Health

Untreated human sewage teems with salmonella, hepatitis, dysentery, cryptosporidium, and many other infectious diseases. One hundred years ago, epidemics of these diseases helped limit the life expectancy of a U.S. citizen to about 50 years. Estimates vary for how many people sewage still sickens or kills each year, but they are all large.

Public utility workers attempt to clean up a sewage spill in a city creek.

Germs linger even after the stench of sewage has dispersed. Healthy adults may never realize that yesterday's swim caused today's cough, diarrhea, or ear infection. Young children, their grandparents, and people already weakened by illness are more likely to become seriously ill or die. Scientists believe as many as 3.5 million Americans get sick each year after swimming, boating, fishing, or otherwise touching water they thought was safe. A 1998 study published in the

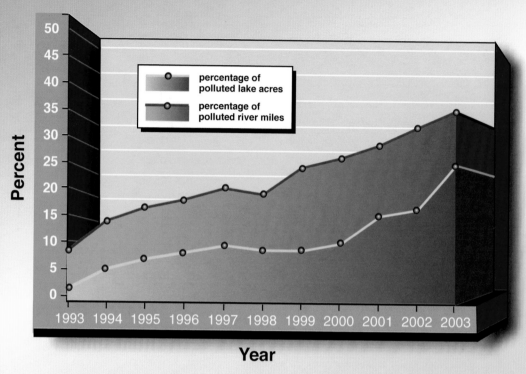

Polluted River Miles and Lake Acres in the United States

Legend:
- percentage of polluted lake acres
- percentage of polluted river miles

Y-axis: Percent
X-axis: Year

Source: U.S. Environmental Protection Agency; *Index of Leading Environmental Indicators 2005,* www.pacificresearch.org, April 2005.

International Journal of Epidemiology blamed water pollution for one-third of all reported gastroenteritis cases and two-thirds of all ear infections.

It's not just the people who play in and around the water who are at risk. Between 1985 and 2000, the Centers for Disease Control (CDC) documented 251 separate disease outbreaks and nearly half a million cases of waterborne illness from polluted drinking water in the United States. Another study by the CDC and the National Academy of Sciences concluded that most illnesses caused by eating tainted seafood have human sewage as the root cause.

The price of sewage spills isn't just measured by the number of illnesses and deaths. Recreational economies like those in Winter Park and Granby, Colo., could suffer if sewage makes the Fraser River (#3 on [2005's] list) unappealing or unsafe to swim and fish in. There are countless rural towns in the same position nationwide.

The prognosis is for these problems to get worse . . . and soon.

Treatment Plants from Yesteryear

To understand why this is happening, it's helpful to know some history. For centuries most American sewage poured into the nearest river or creek with little or no treatment, and few people gave it a second thought. That changed when Congress passed the Clean Water Act in 1972 and the federal government began making significant investments to modernize sewage treatment infrastructure serving communities across the country.

Today, many of the plants built with that initial investment are undersized or are near the end of their effective lives. There are 600,000 miles of sewer pipes across the country and the average age is 33 years. Some pipes in cities along the eastern seaboard are nearly 200 years old. Some are even made of wood. In 2001, The American Society of Civil Engineers gave America's wastewater infrastructure a "D" grade overall.

Runaway Development Today

Poorly planned development compounds the problem of aging infrastructure. As urban areas sprawl into the countryside, new expanses of concrete and asphalt increase the amount of stormwater surging into sewers—and the amount of pollution spewing out.

Consider this: A single acre of wetlands can hold up to 1.5 million gallons of rain or melting snow. When that wetland is replaced by a parking lot or big box store, that water runs off and often winds up in the sewer system. Trees help keep water out of sewer systems, too. In fact, the group American Forests estimates that as Washington, D.C.'s tree canopy thinned by 43 percent between 1973 and 1997, the amount of stormwater running into the city's aging sewer system increased by 34 percent.

In the 1980s and 1990s, a boom in low-density, poorly planned development devoured millions of acres of wetlands, forest, and other habitat across the country. American Rivers estimates that metro Atlanta, for example, now contends with an additional 56 to 132 billion gallons

An environmentalist surveys a deserted beach closed because of sewage contamination.

more stormwater each year than it did before 1982. That's as many as three and a half tanker trucks of polluted water running into the sewer for each resident each year. Older sewage systems combine stormwater with household sewage, but even in systems where they are separated some stormwater ends up in the sewer, where it contributes to raw sewage overflows.

The compounding problems of aging systems and new development are illustrated by Ohio's Little Miami River (#7 on [2005's] list). Cincinnati's Sycamore Creek Sewage Plant can't handle its existing base of customers and has polluted the Little Miami with illegal discharges at least 840 times [from 2000 to 2005]. Adding insult to injury, a proposed bridge across the river would open new areas along the river for development, increasing pressure on the already inadequate facility.

Solution: Invest More to Protect Clean Water

There is no getting around the fact that solving this problem will be expensive. The U.S. Environmental Protection Agency (EPA) estimates that sewer and wastewater treatment capital replacement will cost between $331 and $450 billion, or $17 to $23 billion per year for the next 20 years. Former EPA administrator Christine Todd Whitman warned that without this level of investment, sewage problems could return to 1970s levels by 2016.

This is a job that is too big for states and localities to do on their own, and the public knows it.

"Clean water has no local boundaries. . . . Americans believe this is a national problem and not just a local responsibility," wrote noted pollster Frank Luntz in February 2004. "As they see it, a 21st Century nation should NOT have a 19th Century system to keep their water clean."

EVALUATING THE AUTHOR'S ARGUMENTS:

This viewpoint discusses the role that development plays in decreasing wetlands and forests and increasing pollution. The author argues that the construction of buildings and parking lots contributes to water pollution. In your opinion, what can be done about this problem? What would you recommend to fix environmental problems associated with development?

Water Pollution Is Not a Serious Problem

Jack M. Hollander

"It is not an exaggeration to say that improvements in water quality have been spectacular."

In the following viewpoint Jack M. Hollander argues that water—at least in wealthy, industrialized nations, including the United States—is clean and steadily becoming cleaner. Although there were periods in the twentieth century when American water was highly polluted, he argues, the Clean Water Act of 1972 has led to substantial improvements. In fact, he contends, water is now so clean for wealthy nations that many people have unrealistically high expectations for how much water they should have and how clean it should be.

Until his retirement, Hollander was a professor of energy and resources at the University of California at Berkeley.

AS YOU READ, CONSIDER THE FOLLOWING QUESTIONS:

1. According to the viewpoint, where does freshwater come from?
2. How much has the United States spent on improving water quality since 1972, as reported by Hollander?
3. According to Hollander, how many people could Earth's supply of freshwater sustain?

Jack M. Hollander, *The Real Environmental Crisis: Why Poverty, Not Affluence, Is the Environment's Number One Enemy.* Berkeley and Los Angeles: University of California Press, 2004. Copyright © 2004 by the Regents of the University of California. Reproduced by permission.

W ater is one of the earth's most critical resources. Like air, it is essential to support life. The earth has basically two sources of potable (drinkable) water: freshwater and groundwater. (Salt water from the oceans, although unlimited in amount, is not potable unless the salt is removed, a very expensive process.) Freshwater comes from precipitation—rain, snow, and sleet. Although freshwater is a truly renewable resource, its replenishment depends on annual precipitation, which is not only bounded in amount but also varies from year to year. . . .

Because water is so basic a resource, it poses many issues for society— issues of supply, distribution, cost, quality. As with other resources, the dimensions of these water problems are quite different in rich and poor countries. The water policies and practices of the affluent societies have

Lake Erie, one of the U.S. Great Lakes, was so polluted in 1970 it was deemed dead.

New Jersey officials report at a 2002 news conference that the state's once-polluted shoreline now tests as one of the nation's cleanest.

been moving in the right direction for some time. In the United Kingdom, for example, the government has established national priorities for ground-water management "to protect a priceless national asset." Most other affluent countries have set similar priorities and have seen major improvements in their water systems. . . .

Rising Expectations

It would be difficult to exaggerate the contrast between the water quality standards of the affluent countries and those of most developing countries. In the United States and other industrialized countries, serious water-quality problems are rare and, with steadily increasing water-quality standards, will be even rarer in the future. Throughout the twentieth century, local water-purification systems were widely employed in the United States and generally provided Americans with drinking water of very high quality. Nonetheless, periods of intense industrial growth brought a variety of troublesome water-pollution problems. With the enormous increases of industrial production during and after World War II, pollution of U.S. waterways and lakes greatly increased. By the end of the 1960s, water pollution was almost ubiquitous. A famous example is Lake Erie, whose beaches and fishing facilities were mostly closed down by 1970 and whose tributary river, the Cuyahoga, carried so much industrial and household debris that it actually caught fire in 1969. Another example is the Potomac River, which carried raw sewage through the nation's capital for years and whose estuary was shunned by fall-migrating waterfowl for about fifteen winters.

In 1972 the country's first landmark water-quality legislation was passed by Congress. In the years since passage of the Clean Water Act, the United States has invested over $100 billion in water quality. It is not an exaggeration to say that improvements in water quality have been spectacular. In 1972 only 30–40 percent of assessed waters met water quality goals such as being safe for fishing and swimming, but by 1988 60–70 percent were safe. In 1972 wetland losses were estimated at 460,000 acres per year, whereas at present they are only about one-fourth of that rate. Since 1982, soil erosion from cropland has been reduced by more than a third, substantially reducing sediments, nutrients, and other pollutants that reach streams, lakes, and rivers. In 1972 only 85 million people were served by sewage treatment plants; by now [2004] fourteen thousand new facilities have been built and 173 million people are served. Not only do such plants exist, but the entire country now has uniform treatment standards for sewage plants. Annual discharges of conventional industrial pollutants have been reduced by over 100 million pounds, and toxic pollutants by 24 million pounds. And in 1998, 89 percent of the U.S. population was served by community drinking-water systems reporting no health standard violations.

FAST FACT

Since the Clean Water Act was passed in 1972, the amount of oil spilled annually into the nation's waterways has decreased by 90 percent, according to a report by William Andreen of the University of Alabama School of Law.

Grounds for Optimism

This remarkable progress in water quality, achieved in just a few decades by the United States and by other affluent countries, provides grounds for optimism regarding the possibility of bringing high-quality water supplies to people everywhere. The world's freshwater supply is plentiful, more than adequate to sustain a healthy life for nine billion or more people. In the coming decades technological innovations will potentially increase both water quality and efficient water use, while new institutional arrangements will increasingly reflect the true societal and economic value of water.

But making real progress has other conditions as well. First, planning for future water requirements by local and regional governments needs to become more realistic, framed not in traditional projections of ever higher water "needs" but rather in terms of actually available water. Second, expanded international cooperation programs are essential to promote more equitable development and distribution of water resources. Third and perhaps most important, growing investments of financial and human resources, both public and private, must be dedicated over the coming decades to solving the world's water problems.

Challenges Remain

Although much has been achieved in the United States in improving water quality and availability, the progress is not sufficient in the context of the constantly rising expectations and priorities of a very affluent society. Many challenges remain for reaching the level of water quality that Americans want and deserve. Most of the country's coastal waters need protecting and restoring. The continuing loss of wetlands, though much lower than in the 1970s and 1980s, must be further slowed. The water quality of lakes, rivers, estuaries, and entire watersheds must be improved so they meet all water-quality goals. Chemical and microbial contaminants in drinking water, some of which pose increasing threats to public health and wildlife habitat, must be further lowered.

Although to most Americans these goals are regarded as imperative, they could understandably be judged as esoteric, remote, and perfectionist in the context of the appalling water conditions that still

A young girl plays in polluted water in Haiti, one of many poor countries where clean water is in short supply.

afflict billions of the world's poor people. Thus, in its totality, the water issue provides a clear illustration of the huge gap between the environmental perceptions and priorities of the rich and of the poor. Water also illustrates how societal expectations of environmental quality continually rise as affluence rises. That is how it should be. Nonetheless, the exaggerated rhetoric of environmental catastrophe that pervades the affluent societies reveals a certain insensitivity to the importance of these rich–poor differences. It would be unfortunate if this rhetoric has the overall effect of deflecting attention from the world's really critical environmental problem—poverty.

EVALUATING THE AUTHOR'S ARGUMENTS:

The viewpoint you have just read describes two important reasons that water quality improved in the United States during the twentieth century: new technology for purifying water and new laws to prohibit pollution. What do you think prevents poorer countries from following the example of the United States? What might be some reasons that billions of people are still without clean water?

Chapter 2

How Does Pollution Affect Public Health?

Hong Kong tourists see only the city's growing air pollution from a not-so-scenic overlook.

Air Pollution Has Increased Asthma Cases

Gina Solomon, Elizabeth H. Humphreys, and Mark D. Miller

"The increase in the rate of asthma and its severity almost certainly results from environmental, rather than genetic, factors."

In the following viewpoint Gina Solomon, Elizabeth H. Humphreys, and Mark D. Miller argue that environmental factors, particularly air pollution, have caused the increase in asthma that has occurred in the United States over the past two decades. They discuss a variety of chemicals and contaminants found in the air and their effect on the human body. They cite evidence that suggests that these pollutants trigger asthma attacks in people already diagnosed with asthma and even cause the disease in healthy people. They conclude that environmental factors are more significant than heredity in causing an increase in asthma.

The authors of this viewpoint are physicians who specialize in the care of children. Solomon and Miller work with the University of California at San Francisco Pediatric Environmental Health Specialty Unit, and Humphreys is a pediatrics resident at the University of California at San Francisco.

Gina Solomon, Elizabeth H. Humphreys, and Mark D. Miller, "Asthma and the Environment: Connecting the Dots," *Contemporary Pediatrics*, vol. 21, August 2004, pp. 73–80. *Contemporary Pediatrics* is a copyrighted publication of Advanstar Communications, Inc. All rights reserved. Reproduced by permission.

AS YOU READ, CONSIDER THE FOLLOWING QUESTIONS:
  1. Why, according to the authors, can genetic factors not be the cause of the rapidly increasing rate of asthma?
  2. What evidence do the authors present that emissions from cars and trucks lead to asthma attacks?
  3. Which ethnic group in the United States is most prone to developing asthma, according to the viewpoint?

Asthma affects between 17 and 26 million people in the United States, nearly a third of whom are children. Many studies have reported that asthma is increasing in the US and around the world, with a dramatic increase in young children. Despite greater awareness of the disease and improvements in treatment, the reported prevalence of asthma among children increased by 58% between 1982 and 1992, and deaths directly attributable to asthma increased by 78% from 1980 to 1993. The odds of an adverse outcome (such as intubation, cardiopulmonary arrest, or death) among children hospitalized for asthma in California doubled between 1986 and 1993.

There is widespread consensus among experts that the increases in asthma are real, and not solely the result of greater awareness of the disease. Possible explanations for the increase in prevalence and severity include environmental exposures. . . .

Pediatricians play a significant role in managing and treating asthma, which should include counseling patients and families about potentially preventable environmental exposures that can cause or exacerbate [the] disease. Moreover, armed with accumulating evidence regarding environmental exposures in children, pediatricians can serve as effective community advocates for a healthy environment.

Genes Do Not Explain Asthma Increases

Asthma has both genetic and environmental components. Atopic people [those with inherited sensitivity] are more likely to develop allergies, eczema, and asthma. In fact, 28% of children whose mothers have asthma have themselves been diagnosed with asthma, compared to only 10% of children of nonasthmatic mothers. It is clear, however, that the rapidly increasing rate of asthma in the population cannot be

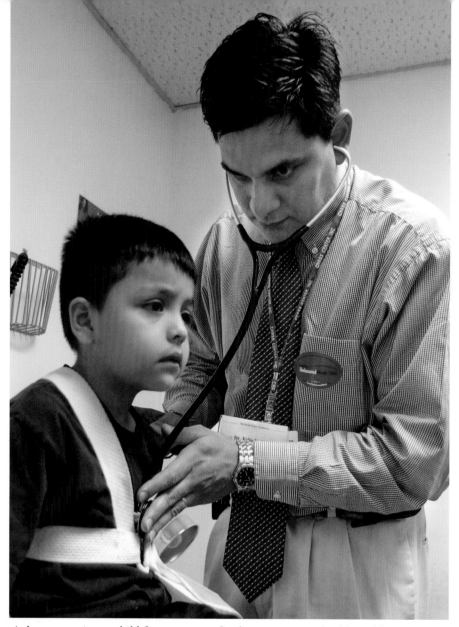

A doctor examines a child for symptoms of asthma, a growing health problem among children.

caused by genetic changes because genetic changes occur over many generations. In addition, asthma is increasing among people without atopy or a family history of allergic disease.

Air Pollutants That Cause Asthma
Environmental exposures are known to trigger attacks in people with asthma. Recent research indicates that such exposures may actually

cause asthma in some people. Environmental factors associated with asthma include viral infection, contaminants in indoor air—such as pet dander, dust mites, cockroach feces, fungal contamination, volatile organic compounds (VOCs), and secondhand smoke—and pollen and common pollutants (ozone, nitrogen oxides, particulate matter, diesel exhaust) in outdoor air. Some chemicals—such as isocyanates, methacrylates, epoxy resins, some pesticides, some types of wood dust, and bacterial toxins—can cause or contribute to asthma. Although they are most often associated with occupational asthma, some of them also may be found in the home.

Recent research has begun to uncover important changes in immune function that can set the stage for asthma very early in life. Some researchers have discovered that fetuses can become sensitized to environmental contaminants before birth, emerging with a strong predisposition to allergy and asthma. Some, but not all, studies have found that breastfed infants are less likely to develop asthma and allergy than babies who are fed formula. Scientists believe that immune modulators in breast milk can help the infant's immune system develop in a way that decreases susceptibility to infectious disease and allergy. . . .

Truck Traffic and Engine Exhaust

Asthma is more common in urban areas of industrialized countries, particularly among children living along busy roads and trucking routes. A population-based survey of more than 39,000 children in Italy found that those who lived on streets with heavy truck traffic were 60% to 90% more likely to have acute and chronic respiratory symptoms such as wheezing or phlegm and illnesses such as bronchitis and pneumonia. A German study of more than 3,700 adolescent students found that those who lived on a street with "constant" truck traffic were 71% more likely to report hay fever–like symptoms and more than twice as likely to report wheezing. Studies also have shown that the proximity of a child's school to major roads

> **FAST FACT**
>
> The Centers for Disease Control and Prevention estimate that American students miss 14 million school days each year because of asthma. Adults miss about 12 million workdays.

is linked to asthma and that the severity of asthmatic symptoms increases with proximity to truck traffic.

Both nitrogen oxides and particulate matter have been linked to a significant decrease in growth of lung function among children living in southern California. Although some components of outdoor air pollution have been declining in the US, ozone and fine particle pollution (PM2.5) from diesel engine exhaust are an ongoing and increasing problem.

Outdoor Air Pollutants

Numerous studies have demonstrated an association between specific components in outdoor air and asthma attacks. Pollen and mold levels, for example, are associated with asthma exacerbations. Among air pollutants, particulates have been linked to increases in emergency

A young girl suffering an asthma attack waits with her mother while receiving treatment at an emergency room.

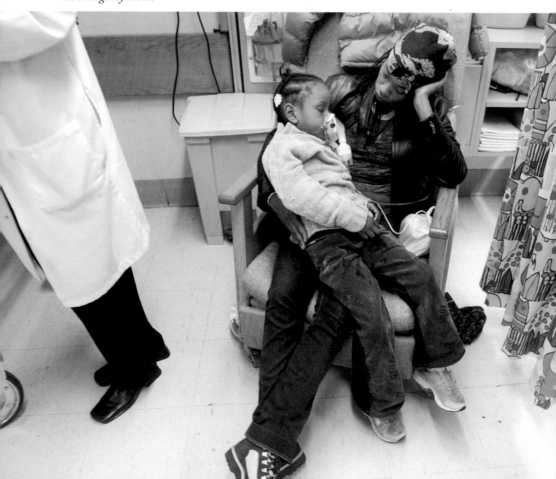

In Atlanta, Georgia, a freeway sign warns drivers of a smog alert and encourages carpooling to reduce pollution.

room visits for asthma. Nitrogen dioxide (NO_2) and sulfur dioxide directly damage the respiratory system. Exposure to sulfur dioxide in laboratory volunteers results in airway constriction, chest tightness, and asthmatic symptoms. Elevated levels of NO_2 in outdoor air are associated with exacerbations of asthma. Because these compounds are potent airway irritants, it is not surprising that they can trigger asthma attacks. . . .

New data suggest that air pollutants such as diesel exhaust and ozone may actually cause asthma in previously healthy children. Diesel exhaust is a major source of ambient PM2.5 and NO_2. It has been associated with asthma causation by several lines of evidence. . . .

A prospective study of more than 3,500 nonasthmatic school children growing up in southern California found that children who exercised outdoors and lived in an area with a smog problem were at increased risk of developing asthma. In communities with a high ozone concentration, children who played three or more sports faced an asthma risk 3.3 times higher than their peers who played no sports. Sports had no effect in areas of low ozone concentration. In general, time spent outdoors was associated with a 40% higher incidence of asthma in areas of high ozone but not in low-ozone areas. . . .

Asthma is an illness that has been increasing in frequency and severity among children in most developed countries. It is most common in African-American children who live in an urban area. Although it is clear that some people inherit a genetic predisposition to asthma, the increase in the rate of asthma and its severity almost certainly results from environmental, rather than genetic, factors.

EVALUATING THE AUTHORS' ARGUMENTS:

In the viewpoint you just read, the authors present evidence that suggests that air pollution has increased asthma rates. How does the fact that the authors are doctors affect the weight you give their views? Explain your answer.

Air Pollution Has Not Increased Asthma Cases

Joel Schwartz

"Air pollution . . . is not a plausible cause of rising asthma."

In the following viewpoint Joel Schwartz argues that the recent increase in asthma has not been caused by air pollution. Air pollution has been decreasing, he contends, so it cannot have led to an increase in asthma. In fact, he points out that children living in the most polluted area of the country seem to develop less asthma than children breathing cleaner air. While it seems reasonable that air pollution might lead to increased asthma, he concludes, the evidence does not support that conclusion.

Joel Schwartz is a visiting scholar at the American Enterprise Institute, a conservative think tank. He is the author of *No Way Back: Why Air Pollution Will Continue to Decline.*

AS YOU READ, CONSIDER THE FOLLOWING QUESTIONS:

1. What reasons does Schwartz suggest for the recent rise in asthma cases?

Joel Schwartz, "Asthma and Air Pollution," American Enterprise Institute for Public Policy Research, September 26, 2005. Copyright © 2005 by the American Enterprise Institute for Public Policy Research. Reproduced by permission of *The American Enterprise, a National Magazine of Politics, Business, and Culture* (TAEMAG.com).

The prevalence of asthma rose by about 75 percent overall between 1980 and 1996, and by nearly a factor of two in children up to 17 years of age. Prevalence seems to have leveled off since then. Roughly 6 to 7 percent of American children currently have asthma.

What caused this large rise in asthma over the last few decades? One hypothesis is that people no longer get as many infections and other immune challenges in childhood, and that this somehow makes them more susceptible to allergic diseases such as asthma. Obesity is also associated with a greater risk of developing asthma and the prevalence of obesity has been increasing. Increasing indoor exposures to allergens may also play a role, as people spend more time indoors and in buildings with better insulation from outside air. These hypotheses are the subject of continuing research.

However, among the potential causes of asthma, none has received as much popular attention as air pollution. Each year, dozens of news stories, reports by environmental groups and regulatory agencies, and scientific and medical journal articles claim or imply that air pollution plays a major role in whether a person develops asthma. Are they right? We need to distinguish two questions here. First, can air pollution cause people to develop asthma? Second, could air pollution be responsible for the rise in the prevalence of asthma during the last few decades?

Air Pollution Is Declining

The second question has a straightforward answer. Air pollution, at least the wide range of air pollutants we measure, is not a plausible cause of rising asthma. Air pollution of all kinds has been declining at the same time asthma has been rising. . . .

California data for four pollutants—ozone, particulate matter under 10 microns (PM10), nitrogen dioxide (NO_2), and carbon monoxide

(CO)—whose ambient levels are regulated by federal standard . . . have . . . been declining, [as have been] sulfur dioxide, lead, and PM2.5.

California measures other pollutants as well, . . . [such as] benzene, 1,3-butadiene, and benzo(a)pyrene. The first two are gases emitted mainly by gasoline engines. The third is an organic particulate emitted by diesel engines. All three have been going down at all sites where they are measured. Other air pollutants that have been declining include the gases acetaldehyde, xylene, perchloroethylene, methylene chloride, trichloroethylene, and styrene, and the particulates dibenz(a,h)anthracene, benzo(b)fluoranthene, and hexavalent chromium.

I used data from California because it has one of the most extensive pollution monitoring networks in the country. But you could just as easily perform the same exercise in any other state and get the same result—declining air pollution, rising asthma.

A child gets a checkup in Southern California, where heavy air pollution may put her health at risk.

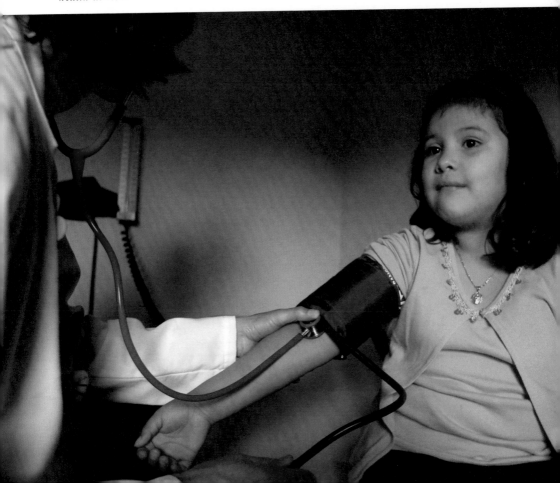

Air Pollution Is an Unlikely Culprit

Even though air pollution isn't responsible for the rise in asthma, could air pollution cause at least some people to develop asthma? The trend data suggest that air pollution is at worst a minor factor. If air pollution had been causing a substantial fraction of all asthma cases in the past, then the large declines in air pollution over the last few decades should have resulted in a large reduction in asthma prevalence, rather than the large increase that actually occurred.

A potential objection to this line of reasoning is that air pollution could be a major cause of asthma, but that some other potent asthma-causing factor(s) increased at the same time air pollution declined, masking the asthma benefits from air pollution reductions. But this hypothesis doesn't wash either. Compared to the 1980s, air pollution was far higher during the 1960s and 70s and was far higher still in previous decades. Yet these "industrial doses" of air pollution in the past were not accompanied by high rates of asthma. Furthermore, many developing countries have much higher air pollution than is ever found in the U.S., yet these countries have much lower rates of asthma than the U.S. or other western countries.

Interpreting Air Pollution Studies

Another way to assess the relationship between air pollution and asthma is to follow a group of children over time in areas with different pollution levels and see how many children develop asthma. This was the premise of the Children's Health Study (CHS) in California. Funded by the California Air Resources Board (CARB), the study followed a few thousand children in 12 different California communities throughout the 1990s. The 12 communities ranged from areas along California's Central Coast that have hardly any air pollution, to areas in southern California with the highest pollution levels in the country.

Researchers from the University of Southern California (USC), who ran the CHS, published their asthma results in 2002 in the journal *Lancet*. The results are surprising. Children living in the six communities with the highest ozone levels were 30 percent less likely to develop asthma than children living in the six lowest-ozone communities. Children living in communities with the highest NO_2, PM10, PM2.5, and acid aerosol levels were 20 percent less likely to develop asthma.

The only suggestion that air pollution could cause asthma came when the researchers looked only at those children who played three or more team sports (8 percent of children in the study). In the four highest ozone communities, these children were more than 3 times as likely to develop asthma as similar children in the other eight communities. The sample size was small, so this result should be viewed with caution. Across the 12 communities, 273 children played three or more team sports, and 29 developed asthma.

More Air Pollution, Less Asthma Risk

Yet even if this relationship between ozone and asthma was causal, it has no general implications for Americans. The study was based on

A scientist compares levels of particulate pollution in the local air.

An inhalation therapist tests an asthmatic child's breathing.

ozone levels during 1994–97 in the highest-ozone areas of southern California. No other area of the U.S. has ever had ozone levels as high as these California communities did during 1994–97. Even the study areas themselves now have much lower ozone levels.

Also keep in mind that the apparent increase in asthma with higher ozone applied only to the children who played three or more team sports. Asthma declined with higher ozone exposure for all other children. Thus, if we believe the CHS was uncovering causal relationships between air pollution and asthma, then the take-home message from the study is that higher air pollution reduces the risk of developing asthma. . . .

The Environmentalist Agenda

If air pollution is causing asthma, it doesn't appear that any of the wide range of substances we measure or regulate could be the culprit. The asthma–air pollution link has medical plausibility, but there doesn't seem to be much support for it in the actual data. The most likely reason for its persistence is its political appeal for environmentalists and regulators. Environmentalists and regulators depend on public fear and outrage over air pollution for their funding, jobs, and power. Claiming that air pollution causes asthma serves their needs by linking air pollution to a serious disease suffered by millions of children.

By pursuing their parochial interests under the guise of public health, environmentalists and regulators are diverting attention and resources from the search for the real causes of and cures for this debilitating disease.

EVALUATING THE AUTHOR'S ARGUMENTS:

The authors of the previous viewpoint and this viewpoint both consider data about children who play sports. They agree on what the Children's Health Study (CHS) found, but they disagree about what the findings mean. In your opinion, which viewpoint makes a more convincing case for the link between childhood asthma and sports? Explain your answer.

Viewpoint
3

Mercury Pollution Poses a Serious Health Risk

Katharine Mieszkowski

> *"Both the brains and nervous systems of children who have been exposed to mercury can be damaged."*

In the following viewpoint Katharine Mieszkowski argues that unborn babies are being exposed to brain-damaging mercury because of fish their mothers eat. Mieszkowski contends that much of the mercury in fish comes from coal-fired power plant emissions. The government is not doing enough to reduce mercury pollution from these plants, she complains. She concludes that warning pregnant women to avoid eating certain kinds of fish is an inadequate response to the dangers posed to children by mercury.

Katharine Mieszkowski is a senior writer for *Salon.com* specializing in technology issues.

AS YOU READ, CONSIDER THE FOLLOWING QUESTIONS:

1. Why, according to pediatrician Kevin Browngoehl, is mercury especially dangerous for the brain of a fetus?

Katharine Mieszkowski, "Mercury Rising," *Salon.com*, April 18, 2005. Reproduced by permission of *Salon*, www.salonmagazine.com.

2. Approximately how many newborns each year have been exposed to mercury, according to the viewpoint?
3. According to the Environmental Protection Agency (EPA), why would eliminating mercury emissions from U.S. power plants not solve the problem?

When children in Dr. Kevin Browngoehl's practice suffer from learning disabilities or attention problems, the pediatrician wonders whether methylmercury in the fish their mothers ate before they were born is to blame. "Once the damage has been done, it appears to be a permanent thing. It's something I can't do much about as a doctor," says Browngoehl, who practices in Drexel Hill, Penn.

Browngoehl explains that mercury travels through a mother's bloodstream, "goes through the placenta, and is concentrated in the brain of the fetus." What's so insidious about the neurotoxin, he says, is that it's likely to present no symptoms in a pregnant woman as it attacks fetal brain cells.

"The mercury is damaging and killing the cells as they're trying to develop areas of the brain that deal with attention and memory," Browngoehl says. "You have a nerve poison being introduced during a critical time of the development of the brain."

Brain-Damaging Effects

Browngoehl's remarks are backed by several alarming studies of mercury in the past decade. One study, sponsored by the U.S. National Institute of Environmental Health Sciences, and Europe's Environment and Climate Research Program, showed that children exposed to mercury in utero [before birth] did poorly on tests measuring their attention span, memory and speaking abilities. According to the U.S. Environmental Protection Agency, both the brains and nervous systems of children who have been exposed to mercury can be damaged. Their language and visual spatial skills can also suffer.

"Children who suffer the consequences of methylmercury toxicity often appear like other children who may have been affected for a genetic reason," explains Leo Trasande, the assistant director of the

Mount Sinai School of Medicine's Center for Children's Health and the Environment in New York. "A child with mental retardation may have had a significant environmental exposure in the perinatal period. But there are no hallmarks." One study found that an affected child could score lower on IQ tests by as little as .20 of a point to as much as 24 points.

The mercury studies are behind the EPA's advisory to moms and would-be moms to avoid eating the most mercury-laden fish, such as swordfish and shark. And to go easy on the tuna. But even with those warnings in place, the agency estimated that as many as 600,000 newborns are being exposed each year. That's 15 percent of the 4 million babies born in the United States each year.

The Fish-Coal Connection

While the [George W.] Bush administration cajoles women to follow its fish warnings, it's proved unwilling to take on the root of the problem. Fish, after all, are only the pathway of mercury to our bloodstreams. Coal-fired power plants, in the United States and abroad, are the largest source of man-made mercury pollution. But Bush and company stand in the way of international efforts to prevent mercury pollution and are doing little to stop it at home.

FAST FACT

The Environmental Protection Agency estimates that approximately 630,000 children are born each year at risk for brain damage because of elevated mercury levels in their mothers' blood.

[In March 2005] the EPA adopted new regulations to curb power plants' emissions of mercury pollution. It heralded its new rules as the very first time that such pollution has been regulated from coal-fired power plants. But environmentalists and health officials view the new rules, which include a pollution trading scheme, as unlikely to make much difference in mercury pollution for more than a decade. "Essentially, the agency adopted a do-nothing approach to mercury for the next 12 years," said John Walke, director of the Natural Resources Defense Council's clean-air program. . . .

Dave Coverly. Reproduced by permission.

The rule calls for mercury pollution from power plants to be reduced 29 percent from 2005 levels by 2010, and 70 percent by 2018. But it also introduces a so-called cap-and-trade program, which will allow power plants to earn credits for larger reductions they make earlier. They can sell these credits to other polluters or bank them for later use. In the proposed rule, the cap on mercury in 2010 was 34 tons. In the final rule, the power plants can continue to emit 38 tons of mercury until 2010. . . .

For its part, the EPA maintains that even if it eliminated all the mercury pollution from U.S. power plants, it still wouldn't clean

Coal-fired power plants like this one are blamed for increased mercury levels in the environment.

up the fish that Americans eat, since the fish supply is so global. "Airborne mercury knows no boundaries; it is a global problem," said acting administrator Steve Johnson in a statement. "Until global mercury emissions can be reduced—and more importantly, until mercury concentrations in fish caught and sold globally are reduced—it is very important for women of child-bearing age to pay attention to the advisory issued by EPA and FDA [Food and Drug Administration], avoiding certain types of fish and limiting their consumption of other types of fish."

So, for the moment, fish eaters will just have to fend for themselves.

Advice for Mothers-To-Be

Karen Perry, deputy director of the environmental health department at Physicians for Social Responsibility, has this advice: "For women who are of child-bearing age, we would advise they learn more about which fish are the cleanest and the safest and continue to eat fish in moderation and choose the lowest-mercury fish. The sad part of all of this is that fish is such a healthy food, we don't want to tell people not to eat it. So you have to give them more information, so they can make the best choices."

But even this type of "throw up your hands and save yourself" advice doesn't sit well with physicians who know that such recommendations

Environmentalists protest rising mercury levels, especially in fish, which is an important food source.

alone won't solve the larger public health issue of what mercury is doing to kids. "It's important to advise families about high mercury levels in fish, but it's unconscionable to not reduce mercury levels in fish," says Trasande from Mount Sinai. "Otherwise, we'll be allowing mercury to poison a generation of our nation's children."

"Think of another disease that you could prevent that affects 600,000 patients in the U.S. a year," says Dr. Browngoehl. "Talk about No Child Left Behind! If you don't want to leave them behind, get the mercury out."

EVALUATING THE AUTHOR'S ARGUMENTS:

This viewpoint begins and ends with passionate quotations from a physician who works with children, and has several quotations from other physicians and researchers. The next viewpoint has only one short quotation and relies more heavily on statistics for its argument. Does this difference affect how you respond to either viewpoint? Explain your answer.

Mercury Pollution Does Not Pose a Serious Health Risk

Sandy Szwarc and Henry I. Miller

> *"American women 'simply are not exposed to levels of methylmercury that would place the newborn children at risk.'"*

In the following viewpoint Sandy Szwarc and Henry I. Miller refute claims that mercury levels in fish are dangerous for humans, particularly for pregnant women and their babies. Scientific studies, they argue, have been unable to find evidence that mercury levels in fish are high enough to cause harm. Pressure from activists to limit mercury emissions from power plants, they conclude, are costly and wasteful, based more on fear than on science.

Sandy Szwarc is a registered nurse who writes about food and dieting. Henry I. Miller is a fellow at the Hoover Institution and the Competitive Enterprise Institute and coauthor of *The Frankenfood Myth: How Protest and Politics Threaten the Biotech Revolution.*

AS YOU READ, CONSIDER THE FOLLOWING QUESTIONS:
1. According to the viewpoint, how do scientists know how much mercury was in fish hundreds of years ago?
2. How do the levels of exposure to mercury suggested by the Environmental Protection Agency (EPA) compare with suggestions in other countries around the world?
3. What does the word *surrogate* mean in the context of the viewpoint?

Environmental activists claim that some fish contain high levels of methylmercury that threaten human health. Unless human consumption of fish is limited, say the activists, pregnant women could be endangering their unborn babies and mothers could be harming their children's developing nervous systems.

The only cases in the scientific literature of mercury poisoning from fish, and subsequent neurological problems, were the result of an industrial mercury spill in Japan in the 1950s. The methylmercury levels in fish resulting from the spill were 40 to 1,000 times higher than the levels found in fish consumed by Americans.

Mercury Levels: Harmless and Dropping

Methylmercury has always been found naturally in fish and in our bodies. The trace levels humans are exposed to have not increased in centuries—in fact, they are dropping. Measurements of 200-year-old fish samples at the Smithsonian Institution and of 550-year-old Alaskan mummies found methylmercury levels many times higher than they are today.

Still, endeavoring to take every precaution to assure the health of babies and children, scientists recently completed two of the most comprehensive, state-of-the-art studies on methylmercury ever conducted. After nearly 15 years, the researchers were unable to find evidence that the amounts of methylmercury in fish eaten by American pregnant women and children put them or the women's newborn infants at risk. Even among populations eating 10 or more times the amount of fish consumed by Americans, scientists have found no credible evidence of neurotoxicity, let alone brain damage, developmental delays, retardation, or learning disabilities.

Although the evidence should provide reassurance, activists and government officials remain unconvinced. They persist in telling women that there is real risk in exceeding U.S. Environmental Protection Agency–established thresholds of methylmercury exposure that were set with extremely conservative safety margins.

A researcher releases a loon at a Maine lake after testing its blood for mercury.

EPA Levels Are Extremely Conservative

To determine acceptable levels of methylmercury, the EPA began with an amount at which there was no observed effect at all in the most sensitive of the population with a lifetime of exposure—a methylmercury level nearly 10 times that found in American women. The EPA then added another 10-fold safety cushion. The resulting safety margins are the most restrictive in the world: On the basis of the same available data, most other scientific agencies in the United States and around the world have established much higher minimum exposure levels. The EPA routinely uses highly conservative (and often dubious) assumptions of safety and extrapolations from high-dose animal

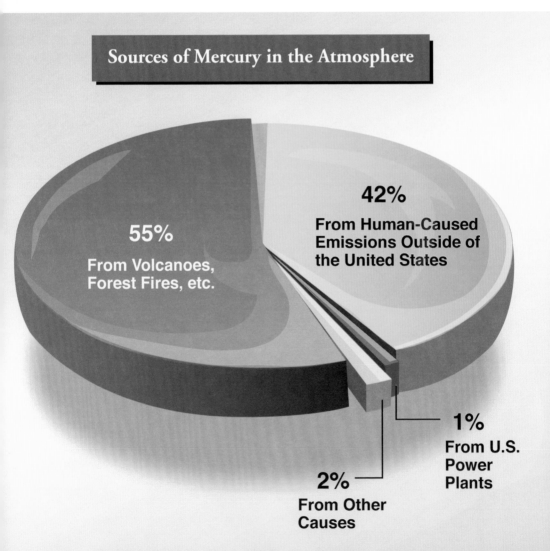

Sources of Mercury in the Atmosphere

55% From Volcanoes, Forest Fires, etc.

42% From Human-Caused Emissions Outside of the United States

1% From U.S. Power Plants

2% From Other Causes

testing to very low chronic exposures in humans, then applies a safety margin of several orders of magnitude to allow for differences between animals and humans, and for possible enhanced susceptibility of pregnant women and children.

When the U.S. Centers for Disease Control and Prevention studied mercury levels in American women of childbearing age and young children, it found not a single woman or child with levels anywhere near those theorized to be unsafe. The U.S. Department of Agriculture's Human Nutrition Information Services (HNIS) also analyzed the diets of American women of childbearing years using several surveys. They then considered every possible circumstance that could raise exposure, including heavy fish consumption, eating fish with the highest methylmercury levels, repeatedly eating the same fish (such as canned tuna), and the amounts of methylmercury in a range of commercial fish samples. But try as they might, they found that it was inconceivable for an expectant mother to eat quantities of fish sufficient to harm her baby. According to Dr. James Heimbach, former associate administrator of the HNIS, American women "simply are not exposed to levels of methylmercury that would place the newborn children at risk."

> **FAST FACT**
>
> Jozef Pacyna of the Norwegian Institute of Air Research concludes in a 2004 study that between 1990 and 2000 the annual amount of human-caused mercury emissions in the United States decreased by 69 tons, from about 176 tons to 107 tons.

The Politics of Mercury

If methylmercury in fish is not a bona fide public health issue in the way that activists and regulators are spinning it, what is the hubbub really about?

The methylmercury issue is merely a surrogate for broader issues relating to emissions from coal-fired power plants. Environmental groups advocated Maximum Achievable Control Technology regulations that would have required utility plants to install available emissions control devices immediately. Selecting the lesser of two public

President George W. Bush (left) watches as a sample of water is taken to test for pollution.

policy evils, the [George W.] Bush administration EPA opted for a cap-and-trade approach under which regulators set overall emissions goals and let markets and human ingenuity figure out how to achieve the target. Individual facilities are permitted flexibility to determine the best technology to meet the restrictions.

But how cost-effective will the new regulations be? How much will those emissions regulations reduce the methylmercury levels in the fish we eat? Certainly much less than consumers are being led to believe. Even the most optimistic estimates suggest that the proposed plans will reduce average methylmercury levels in seafood by no more than 1.7 parts per billion. The insignificance of this reduction, which will have virtually no impact on public health, illustrates just how removed from reality this issue has become.

EVALUATING THE AUTHORS' ARGUMENTS:

The authors of this viewpoint claim that although American women do not eat enough mercury to harm their babies, government officials continue to warn against eating too much fish. In your opinion, what should the government do when evidence seems inconclusive? Should it warn people about possible dangers, even though some people might be unnecessarily frightened? Or should it wait for conclusive evidence before warning people to change their behavior?

Herbicides and Pesticides Pose a Serious Health Risk

Wendy Munson Scullin

"Homeowners end up breathing, eating and absorbing herbicides through their skin as they relax at home."

In the following viewpoint Wendy Munson Scullin warns that the chemicals put on lawns to kill weeds and insects may also prove harmful to people. She argues that, even when used carefully, these chemicals end up inside homes through normal human activity, especially the playful activities of children. She worries that not enough research has been done on exposure to homeowners. Studies of pesticide and herbicide use by farmers and golf course caretakers, for example, have shown that prolonged exposure can cause cancer. Scullin concludes that the risk of toxic exposure is great enough that people should reconsider the value of having the perfect lawn.

Scullin is a freelance writer who has studied horticulture and native plants. She lives in Iowa.

AS YOU READ, CONSIDER THE FOLLOWING QUESTIONS:

1. According to Matthew Wilson, how long did people use the insecticide diazinon before it was banned?

Wendy Munson Scullin, "Keep Off the Grass! The Modern American Lawn Is a Chemical Nightmare, but Alternatives Abound," *E: The Environmental Magazine,* vol. 16, May/June 2005. Copyright © 2005. Reproduced by permission of *E: The Environmental Magazine.*

2. Why, according to Dr. Philip Landrigan, are children especially at risk from toxic exposure to herbicides and pesticides?
3. Why does the author say that weed killers "are a reaction to a preventable problem"?

Thirty years ago, Doris Goodwin was doing something she loved to do: working in her yard. She owned three acres of wooded land, gardens and lawn in New York's Hudson Valley, which sometimes proved a challenge to maintain. For years, she had faithfully applied a cocktail of herbicides and pesticides on trouble spots, always being careful to follow directions and use safety equipment. But this time, something went wrong. Goodwin accidentally inhaled a toxic dose of herbicides, and it immediately felled her.

Goodwin was significantly impaired for about six months, and it took about a year for her to return to some semblance of normalcy. After the acute poisoning, Goodwin developed asthma, and spent the remaining 25 years of her life with headaches, decreased energy and a newfound sensitivity to a wide range of chemicals she'd used around the home for years. She was no longer able to tolerate conventional herbicides because of adverse reactions, and was forced to switch to natural lawn techniques for the rest of her life.

Studies Cannot Keep Up with Toxins

Chemicals that have known toxic or carcinogenic effects are still on the market, as evidence continues to mount and long-term studies proceed. "There simply has not been adequate testing to show the true dangers of herbicides and pesticides," argues Matthew Wilson, director of the New England–based Toxics Action Center. Wilson points to the recent Environmental Protection Agency (EPA) ban of the popular insecticide diazinon as an example of how slow the regulatory process can be. "Everyone used diazinon for 20 or 25 years, but it wasn't until testing in the late 1990s showed it to be harmful that it got banned," he says.

Still, if we had a choice we might err on the side of caution and the so-called precautionary principle, which says that chemicals should not be used until they've been thoroughly studied, critics argue. "The pesticide industry has significant influence on government," says Wilson.

Chemicals on the Move
Herbicide makers argue that the majority of their products applied to grass stays there. But what about the rest of it? Some gets washed into ground and surface waters, threatening natural systems. You track some into the house on your shoes, according to a study by the National Exposure Research Laboratory and the EPA. Kids, pets and wildlife can't read those little flags that warn, "stay off until dry," and the warnings may in any case be inadequate. "Twenty-four hours of drying time is no assurance," says Wilson, "because the time it takes lawn chemicals to break down varies greatly. Some stay for a long time."

Removing shoes inside the house helps, but there is still the problem of dust. Herbicides become aerosolized, and some particles are small

An Idaho farmworker shows the medication she must take after continued exposure to herbicides.

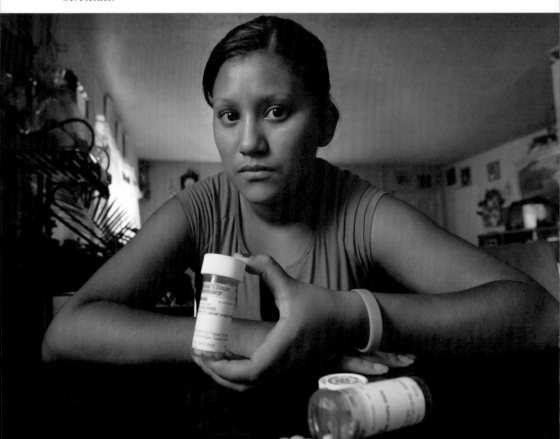

enough (less than 10 microns, the "deadly" PM10s) to infiltrate the lungs. Herbicide dust can enter the house anywhere air can. Plus, these chemicals tend to break down more slowly indoors, since they are exposed to less sunlight and water. The particles lodge in carpets and fabrics, so homeowners end up breathing, eating and absorbing herbicides through their skin as they relax at home. "Tests find DDT [a pesticide] dust in people's homes, even though the chemical had been banned 30 years ago," says Wilson.

Further, as Dr. Philip Landrigan, director of Mount Sinai School of Medicine's Center for Children's Health and the Environment, explains, "Kids' behavior puts them at greater risk—they are on the floor and con-

FAST FACT

According to a study by the Environmental Protection Agency, Americans apply more than 80 million pounds of chemical herbicides and pesticides to their lawns and gardens each year.

stantly have their hands in their mouths." While the amount of lawn chemicals one might take in daily from the home is well below the level the EPA has determined to be risky, would you willingly eat or apply herbicide to your skin (or your children's skin) on a daily basis? What about people who are especially sensitive?

Studying Herbicides' Effect on Health

The herbicide 2,4-D kills plants by overdosing them with growth hormones in a process that is not precisely understood. What happens when humans are exposed to this chemical? Research in Sweden in 1981 found the occurrence of lymphomas (a variety of soft-tissue cancer) to be five times higher than normal in people exposed to 2,4-D-type herbicides. A study of Kansas farmers who applied or prepared 2,4-D for more than 20 days per year identified a non-Hodgkin's lymphoma incidence six times higher than that of the average population. A study in Canada found risks of this cancer increased along with increased exposure to herbicides.

A study by the National Cancer Institute in Iowa and Minnesota did not find significantly elevated risk of cancers in relation to any specific herbicide. But farmers overall tend to experience higher-than-usual occurrences of many types of cancer. Because the farmers in the

Dave Coverly. Reproduced by permission.

Midwestern study were also exposed to pesticides, gas fumes, fertilizers, solvents and fungicides, the researchers had difficulty isolating variables.

According to the National Cancer Institute, "It takes many years for the development of a tumor and even more years until the detection of a tumor and its spread to other parts of the body. People exposed to carcinogens from smoking cigarettes, for example, generally do not develop detectable cancer for 20 to 30 years." This is not necessarily true for all cancers, but it is a common trend. Therefore, studying people with recent exposure to herbicides may not detect carcinogenicity.

For greater clarity, scientists are examining a population that experiences regular, extensive exposure to herbicides over long periods of time—golf course superintendents. Studies at the University of Iowa showed a 23 percent increase in non-Hodgkin's lymphoma, 29 percent increase in prostate cancer, 17 percent increase in cancer of the large intestine, and 20 percent increase in brain and nervous system cancers.

On the other hand, preliminary studies of professional herbicide applicators (*Journal of Environmental Medicine,* 1995) showed no increase in cancers. This study did not allow many years to lapse after exposure, however. Many people held the job for less than one year.

A Healthy Lawn Is Not Worth It

Another interesting piece of the herbicide puzzle is that by merely looking for incidences of cancer, we may be missing part of the picture. In 1996 the *Journal of Occupational Environmental Medicine* reported that farmers who had been exposed to 2,4-D-type herbicides had significantly reduced numbers of immune response cells in their blood. "Further studies should clarify whether the immunological changes found may have health implications," conclude the researchers. In many cases, suppression of the immune system is known to weaken its ability to fight cancer.

What about the low doses of exposure that an average homeowner experiences over time? The short answer is that we simply don't know yet. Short-term effects of 2,4-D exposure can include cough, dizziness, nausea and loss of muscle coordination. This may be as much of a deterrent for some as cancer risks.

Working in her garden may threaten this woman's health if she uses toxic chemicals to kill pests.

People don't tend to think too much about preventing problems—we react to them. Herbicides are a reaction to a preventable problem. . . .

"From our perspective it is not worth the risk to our water, children and pets [to use conventional herbicides]," says Wilson. The advocacy group Beyond Pesticides points out that passing local ordinances restricting, the use of herbicides and pesticides is very difficult, because "41 states, whose legislatures have been subject to chemical industry lobbying have acted to preempt local authority to regulate pesticides." However, there are many ways people can tend beautiful, healthy, functional lawns without a deluge of industrial chemicals. . . .

[But] who needs a lawn, anyway? Some homeowners are simply giving up on green lawns and planting fast-spreading, no-maintenance native covers instead—or simply letting their acreage grow wild (a solution that may run afoul of local zoning ordinances). Another solution is a rock garden or woodland. In 50 years, herbicides have become so ingrained in our culture that we may not think other methods are effective. Trading the ease of applying herbicide for hand pulling weeds and improving your lawn's health takes effort, especially at first. But one day the "perfect lawn" may be redefined as one that is pleasing to look at and safe to live with. An ounce of prevention is worth a pound of herbicide.

EVALUATING THE AUTHOR'S ARGUMENTS:

In this viewpoint the author favors the "precautionary principle," or the idea that we should not use a chemical until it has been thoroughly tested. In the next viewpoint the author argues that applying the precautionary principle to pesticide use could do more harm than good. After reading both viewpoints, which view do you find more convincing? Why?

Viewpoint
6

Herbicides and Pesticides Do Not Pose a Serious Health Risk

Barbara McLintock

"No one needs to panic because the dog is wearing a flea collar and the children are eating lots of [nonorganic] produce."

In the following viewpoint, originally addressed to readers in Canada, Barbara McLintock argues that pesticides do not seriously threaten humans when the pesticides are minimally used. Average families should not panic over exposure to chemicals intended to kill weeds or insects, she says. Nor should they restrict their consumption of fruits and vegetables because they fear being poisoned. She acknowledges that some studies have concluded high levels of exposure to pesticides can be dangerous, but points out that none of these apply to typical family use. In fact, she concludes, most people in North America derive more benefit than harm from herbicides and pesticides.

McLintock is a freelance writer and consultant based in Victoria, Canada. The *Tyee*, in which this viewpoint originally appeared, is an online daily newspaper specializing in investigative stories.

C anadian parents can be forgiven for feeling panic today, convinced that they, or their children, are at grave risk of contracting any one of a number of horrible diseases. The reason? They had applied Weed-N-Feed to combat the dandelions in the lawn, or put a flea collar on the family dog, or even allowed their children to eat non-organic apples that had somehow, somewhere, come into contact with a pesticide.

Overreacting to Poor Studies

The panic, while largely unjustified, stems from a report made public [in 2004] by the Ontario College of Family Physicians, which concluded that pesticides are so toxic that there may well be no safe level of exposure.

Spokespersons for the College spoke of a litany of health problems they believed occurred from pesticide exposure, ranging from various cancers to learning disabilities and depression. They said they would begin to encourage Ontario doctors to advise patients to avoid all pesticide exposures, not even eating food that had been exposed to pesticides if it was at all possible to avoid it.

Their comments were based on a 179-page report prepared by a committee of the College whose members had spent the past year reviewing as many previous studies as they could find on the effects of pesticide exposure on human health. . . .

Although a number of media reports described the work as "the largest study" ever done in Canada on pesticide exposure, the team did not conduct any clinical or epidemiological investigations itself. Its work was limited to reviewing studies others had done.

And therein lies the problem. The team was stuck with those other studies, with any methodological flaws they contained, and most especially with whatever groups it was that those other researchers had chosen to study.

Few Ordinary Families Studied

When their work is studied in detail, it becomes apparent that almost none of the studies used involve ordinary families who put a flea collar on the dog or eat non-organic produce or even use pesticides once or twice a year to get rid of the tent caterpillars on the trees or the weeds in the lawn. Rather, a high proportion of the studies cited involve people who are exposed to pesticides at very high dosages, very frequently, and, far too often, without proper precautions being taken. They are people who work in factories where pesticides are made, or farmworkers who labour day after day among pesticide-laden plants, or golf course workers who are applying herbicides to fairways and greens on a regular basis.

Even worse, many of the workers studied were employed in countries where worker safety regulations are virtually unknown. They were banana workers in Ecuador, pest-control workers in India, potato farmers in

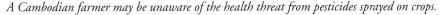

A Cambodian farmer may be unaware of the health threat from pesticides sprayed on crops.

Colombia, to name just a few examples. In some cases, the studies also looked at the children of the farmworkers and pesticide applicators.

Unquestionably, the studies showed that, over-all, those who were subjected to those high levels of exposure were at greater risk of developing some cancers, some reproductive problems, some chromosomal aberrations. Those who conducted the studies were the first to admit that it was extremely difficult, even in those cases, to determine just how great the increase in risk was. That's because it's very hard to winnow out the effects of the pesticide exposure from that of other contaminants to which such workers are exposed, ranging from other chemicals used on farms to animal viruses. All the same, the cumulative results of the studies are certainly strong enough to state that strict regulations should be put in place to protect farmworkers and others who must be exposed to high levels of pesticides in their jobs.

More difficult, however, is to take those findings and try to decide what they could mean for that average homeowner or gardener. The Ontario doctors choose to interpret the data as meaning that any level

A pest control worker wears a mask to keep from inhaling toxic chemicals used to keep mosquitoes under control.

of exposure must, therefore, be dangerous, especially to pregnant women or children.

Accidents, Not Fruits and Vegetables, Are the Big Risk
But that conclusion is not inherent in the studies themselves. Only a very few of the studies suggest any link at all between low-level exposure and health problems.

And not a single one suggests that eating fruits or vegetables that have been treated with pesticides poses a measurable health risk.

Most of the other cases of serious harm cited involve accidental poisonings by pesticides—people, especially small children, who ate or drank relatively large amounts of pesticide because they were unaware of what it was or of the dangers of taking in large amounts of it. The results of those studies stress the importance of storing pesticides where children can't get at them and ensuring they remain clearly labeled in their original containers. (A number of poisoning cases have occurred because people have transferred the pesticides to empty pop bottles for ease of application, but haven't relabeled the bottle to make it clear that it no longer contains Coke or 7-Up.)

FAST FACT

According to the National Center for Food and Agriculture Policy, it would cost the United States more than $14 billion every year to use hand weeding and cultivation instead of herbicides on important food and fiber crops. It costs only about $7 billion a year to use herbicides.

However, in order to reach their conclusion that all pesticides should be avoided in all circumstances, the Ontario doctors are relying on what is known as "the precautionary principle." The report describes this principle: "When an activity raises threats of harm to human health or the environment, precautionary measures should be taken, even if some cause and effect relationships are not fully understood."

When Precautions Do More Harm than Good
In many cases, the precautionary principle can be applied with few unintended negative consequences. But the pesticide study is a good example of where its application could actually cause more health problems than it could ever prevent.

Pesticides can greatly benefit human health where they are used to kill, for instance, insects or rodents that serve as vectors of potentially fatal diseases. Millions of lives are saved in tropical countries by using insecticides to kill mosquitoes that would otherwise spread malaria. Even here in North America, the use of larvicides against mosquitoes may prevent the spread of West Nile virus which has killed hundreds of people across the continent [since 2001]. . . .

More indirectly, the use of pesticides to produce cheaper, more accessible fruits and vegetables over-all produces a significant health benefit. Eating fruits and vegetables protects against some types of cancers. Those who eat lots of fruit and vegetables rather than processed high-fat, high-sugar foods are much less likely to be obese, to contract heart disease and to suffer from adult-onset diabetes. But if someone decides that it is safe to eat only organic produce, their over-all consumption of produce may well decline unless they can afford the significantly higher prices of organic items.

The Ontario family doctors have doubtless done the country a favour by raising awareness of potential problems. No one suggests any more that chemical pesticides should be a first line of defense against any insect or weed infestation.

But a detailed read of the studies also shows that no one needs to panic because the dog is wearing a flea collar and the children are eating lots of produce, even if it isn't all organic.

EVALUATING THE AUTHOR'S ARGUMENTS:

In this viewpoint and the one before, both authors agree that there have not been enough scientific studies of how low-level herbicide and pesticide use affects typical people. However, each author comes to a different conclusion about how people should react to the studies of high-level exposure that have been done. After reading both viewpoints, what bearing do you think the high-level exposure studies should have on the average user of pesticides?

Chapter 3

What Can Be Done About Pollution?

Discarded cell phones are sorted for recycling.

Electronics Recycling Should Be Mandatory

Sheila Davis

"Electronic products . . . contain a lengthy list of toxic chemicals, which cause some serious health effects when they leak out of landfills."

In the following viewpoint Sheila Davis asks the U.S. Senate to adopt laws that require electronics manufacturers to safely recycle discarded products. Because recycling safely is so expensive, she explains, most computers are simply discarded or sent overseas to be recycled in ways that are dangerous for workers. Only the federal government, she argues, can force manufacturers to build cleaner machines and to develop safe recycling programs for them.

Sheila Davis is executive director of the Silicon Valley Toxics Coalition. This viewpoint has been excerpted from her testimony before a Senate committee hearing on electronics waste.

AS YOU READ, CONSIDER THE FOLLOWING QUESTIONS:

1. According to the viewpoint, what percentage of discarded computers are recycled?

Sheila Davis, testimony to the Senate Subcommittee on Superfund and Waste Management, http://epw.senate. gov/109th/Davis_testimony.pdf, U.S. Senate Committee on Environment and Public Works, July 26, 2005. Reproduced by permission of the author.

2. Why is it less expensive for recyclers to send computers to Asia rather than process them in the United States, according to Davis?
3. Why, in the author's opinion, will making manufacturers handle some of their own recycling lead them to change the way they design and build computers?

The problem of electronic waste in the U.S. is becoming critical. Discarded computers and other electronic products are the fastest growing part of the waste stream. And these products contain a lengthy list of toxic chemicals, which cause some serious health effects when they leak out of landfills and into our groundwater, or are incinerated into our air.

But less than ten percent of discarded computers are currently being recycled, with the remainder getting stockpiled or improperly disposed of. Fifty to eighty percent of the e-waste collected for recycling is actually being exported to Asian countries which have no infrastructure to accommodate the hazardous properties of e-waste. Due to horrific working conditions and no labor standards in many of the developing countries where e-waste is sent, women and children are often directly exposed to lead and other hazardous materials when dismantling the electronic products to recover the few valuable parts for resale.

[I have a photo that shows] a woman who works in one of these dismantling shops in Guiyu, China. . . . She has no protective equipment whatsoever. Yet she is about to smash a cathode ray tube [CRT] from a computer monitor in order to remove the copper-laden yoke at the end of the funnel. The glass is laden with lead but the biggest hazard this woman faces here is the inhalation of the highly toxic phosphor-dust coating inside this CRT. The monitor glass is later dumped in irrigation canals and along the river where it leaches lead into the groundwater. The groundwater in Guiyu is completely contaminated to the point where fresh water is trucked in constantly for drinking purposes.

Recycling Is Too Expensive
So why does the computer that I turned in, at a local "recycling" event in California, end up in China, at this woman's workplace? Why didn't my

computer get dismantled and recycled here, like I thought it would? The answer is that the market for recycling e-waste here doesn't work. The materials used in these products are so toxic, it's very expensive to recycle them. There are some "good recyclers" who are actually trying to recycle the products as extensively as technology allows, but this requires manual processing, and protecting workers from exposure to the toxic chemicals is very expensive. The economics just don't work for most recyclers. So they look for the cheaper, low-road solutions, and cream off the parts that there is a local market for, and ship the rest across the ocean to become someone else's problem. Or they use low-wage prison labor for disassembly, which further undermines the chances for a healthy recycling market in this country.

So how do we fix this problem? . . .

Manufacturers Must Change

First we need the products to be easier to recycle. The economics of recycling will NEVER work unless these products are easier, and therefore cheaper, to recycle. Part of that means using less toxic materials. Part of that means designing them so they are more easily disassembled for recycling, without relying on prison labor or women and children in China.

Chinese workers sort through a growing pile of discarded electronics, some of which can be recycled.

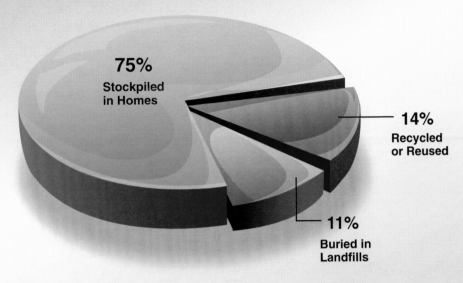

Where Are Obsolete Computers?

75%
Stockpiled
in Homes

14%
Recycled
or Reused

11%
Buried in
Landfills

Source: Dana Joel Gattuso, *Mandated Recycling of Electronics: A Lose-Lose-Lose Proposition*, 2005.

Here's an example of what I mean by designing for easier recycling:

A representative from a printer manufacturer told me a discouraging story about recycling at his company. He said that designers worked with the recyclers and found that if they simply added a $1.25 component part to the new line of printers it would make the printer easier to disassemble and cheaper to recycle. But the design team was told not to include the part because there is no guarantee that the printer would be recycled, so the added cost could not be justified.

So here, the producer was not motivated to change their design because they were not concerned about the recycling end of their product's life.

Manufacturers Must Be Made Legally Responsible

So the second thing we need to do is to get the producers to take responsibility for their products at the end of their useful life, so that they do have this incentive. If the producers (and here I mean the manufacturers and brand owners) have no connection to, or responsibility for, their products at disposal time, then what incentive do they have to modify their designs for better recycling, or even better reuse of their products? The answer is none—they have no incentive to do anything different.

BEING AT THE TOP OF THE EVOLUTIONARY TREE, I SUPPOSE I SHOULD BE MORE CAREFUL

But what if the companies did have responsibility for taking back their products for recycling? What if that was just part of their normal operation, that each company had to recycle a significant portion of its old products each year? They would simply build these takeback and recycling costs into their pricing structure. But to be competitive (and cut their recycling costs), they would innovate, redesign, and end up with computers that were cheaper to recycle. Less toxic materials would be used, so recycling would be easier and cheaper. And there would be no reason to even think about having to use taxpayer money to solve this problem. The market would work.

Taking Care of Electronic Waste

So this is the legislative solution that we are encouraging our lawmakers to adopt, the approach that is called Producer Responsibility. Of course, this is a far reaching, complex solution, with many components that can't be covered in a short testimony. But we think it's the only solution that will correct the market forces that currently send my old computer into a landfill or to a village in China. So my message here today is that this is a big-picture problem that calls for big-picture solutions. It won't be solved with partial fixes like tax breaks or making consumers pay a recycling fee. I encourage our lawmakers to seek the kinds of changes that will actually make the *market* take care of the problem of electronic waste.

EVALUATING THE AUTHOR'S ARGUMENTS:

This viewpoint and the following viewpoint disagree on whether the government should be involved in solving the problem of what to do with discarded electronics. Sheila Davis believes that laws can encourage manufacturers to recycle. Dana Joel Gattuso believes that if the government stays away from the issue of electronics recycling, the market will find the best solution on its own. Which argument is more convincing? Do you think that businesses will find a good environmental solution on their own? Explain your answer.

Electronics Recycling Should Not Be Mandatory

Dana Joel Gattuso

"There is no scientific evidence that e-waste in landfills presents health risks."

In the following viewpoint Dana Joel Gattuso argues that alarm over the disposal of computers and other electronics is unnecessary. She warns that laws to force manufacturers to collect and recycle more computers are based on misinformation about the dangers of simply tossing the machines in landfills. Government intrusion, she concludes, will only make a minor problem into a major one. She predicts it will make both disposal and recycling more difficult and more expensive.

Gattuso is a freelance writer and policy analyst on environmental issues. She previously worked for the U.S. Chamber of Commerce.

AS YOU READ, CONSIDER THE FOLLOWING QUESTIONS:

1. According to the viewpoint, how much extra does a consumer in California pay for a television or a computer in order to help pay for recycling?

2. How much of the U.S. total municipal waste stream is made up of e-waste, according to calculations from the Environmental Protection Agency?
3. How does the cost of recycling computers compare with the cost of disposing of them in landfills?

H aste maketh waste in the fast-paced world of technology. Americans trash two million tons of old computers and other forms of electronic waste every year, according to the Environmental Protection Agency (EPA). While that is a tiny fraction of the nation's total waste stream, the issue is creating heaps of hype and hysteria among state and federal lawmakers about what to do with the "e-waste."

California became the first state to hold consumers responsible for their e-mess. Starting [in 2005], if you buy a television or personal computer [PC] from a manufacturer in California, you will pay $6 to $10 to finance a costly, statewide program to collect and recycle all used monitors. Moreover, manufacturers are required to rethink the way they build computers. By 2007, they must phase out lead—currently used in computers to protect users from the tube's x-rays— mercury, cadmium, and other substances crucial to the operation of PCs.

Maine's law, enacted [in 2004], is even more draconian, requiring manufacturers to arrange and pay to have their used computers and TVs col-

> **FAST FACT**
>
> It costs approximately five hundred dollars to recycle a ton of electronics waste but only about forty dollars to put it in a landfill, according to the Competitive Enterprise Institute.

lected and recycled. Many other states—including Massachusetts, Minnesota, Oregon, Rhode Island, and Texas—are considering legislation similar to California's or Maine's.

Misguided Federal Legislation

Meanwhile, Congress is weighing in to provide a national "solution" and prevent a hodge-podge of 50 different state laws. In January [2005],

Old computer cases line the shelves of a computer recycling center.

Reps. Mike Thompson (D-Calif.) and Louise Slaughter (D-N.Y.) introduced legislation to require consumers to pay a $10 fee on new computer purchases to fund a nationwide e-waste recycling program. While the fee may seem insignificant, there is little reason to believe it would remain low for long; the cost to recycle a single computer is six times that amount.

On March 3 [2005], Sens. Ron Wyden (D-Ore.) and Jim Talent (R-Mo.) introduced the Electronic Waste Recycling Promotion and Consumer Protection Act (S. 510), which would authorize EPA to ban all computer monitors, laptops, and TVs from landfills three years from its enactment. It would also set up a national recycling program by providing tax credits to the recycling industry and to consumers who send their tech trash to a "qualified" recycler. The legislation's sponsors naively assume that tax credits are enough incentive to establish an infrastructure large and strong enough to handle all of the country's computer and TV discards. Furthermore, the bill, if passed, would be disastrous for the nation's numerous voluntary reuse programs. The bill's focus on rewarding recycling would undercut successful and important efforts to refurbish computers for reuse, which has been found to be five to 20 times more energy efficient than recycling. Reuse also makes home computers more affordable.

E-waste Alarmism

This rush to enact some form of costly recycling legislation is the result of a swirl of misinformation spread largely by powerful eco-activist groups—motivated by the belief that the growing amount of electronic waste reflects the ills of a "throw-away" society and that recycling e-waste to achieve "zero waste tolerance" is a moral obligation. Among the myths bandied about are that e-waste is growing at an uncontrollable, "exponential" rate; that, in the words of Sen. Wyden, "growing amounts of e-waste are clogging our nation's landfills"; and that heavy metals contained in computers are leaking out of the landfills, poisoning our soil.

Waste workers sort computers and other electronic equipment at a dump site.

In reality, e-waste has remained at only 1 percent of the nation's total municipal waste stream since EPA began calculating electronics discards in 1999. Furthermore, the annual number of obsolete home computers is expected to level off at 63 million [in 2005]. While that may sound like a lot of computers, it's not an unmanageable amount. If you took all the United States' trash for the next 1,000 years, including e-waste, it would fit into a 120-foot deep, 44 square mile landfill. That's less than one-tenth of 1 percent of the land in the U.S.

Furthermore, landfill capacity is not diminishing but remains constant, according to the EPA. While some landfills have been closing due to stringent federal regulations, they are being replaced with new ones 25 times larger.

Landfill Disposal Is Safe

Finally, there is no scientific evidence that e-waste in landfills presents health risks. Landfills are built today with thick, puncture-resistant liners that keep waste from coming into contact with soil and groundwater. Timothy Townsend of the University of Florida, a leading expert on the effects of electronic waste in landfills, conducted tests in 2003 on 11 landfills containing e-waste from TV and computer monitors mixed in with municipal solid waste. He found concentrations of lead far below the safety standard—and less than 1 percent of what EPA's lab tests had predicted. "There is no compelling evidence," says Townsend, that e-waste creates a risk in landfills.

His conclusions are consistent with findings of other recent studies. A year-long, peer-reviewed study by the Solid Waste Association of North America released [in 2004] concluded that, "extensive data . . . show that heavy metal concentrations in leachate and landfill gas

A worker constructs a new scale at a modern, high-tech landfill.

are generally far below the limits . . . established to protect human health and the environment."

The real problem is that a growing number of state and local regulators, based on misplaced fears, are rushing to ban TVs and PCs from municipal landfills, artificially creating the problem of where to discard them. Mandated recycling is not the answer. The costs, ultimately passed on to consumers, are staggering—$500 per ton of

e-waste to recycle versus $40 per ton to landfill. "Eco-design" require-
ments like California's and Maine's will cripple technological innova-
tion, and substance bans will unleash a host of unintended health and
environmental risks.

Thankfully, there is good news. Manufacturers are recycling their
products on their own, and they're doing it better and cheaper than
government. Hewlett-Packard, Dell, Gateway, and IBM are just a few
of the many manufacturers operating their own recovery programs,
recycling over 160 million pounds of e-waste a year. Equally as prom-
ising is eBay's new "Rethink Initiative" to provide guidance to consumers on recycling, donating, or even selling their used machines
online.

How to make these efforts even more successful? Keep government's
nose out of the e-garbage.

EVALUATING THE AUTHOR'S ARGUMENTS:

In this viewpoint much of the evidence is in the form of
quotations from scientists and statistics from their research.
The previous viewpoint, by Sheila Davis, focuses on the
story of one woman who has been exposed to danger. How
do you respond to these different types of argument—those
relying either on rational or on emotional appeals? Which
do you find more persuasive? Explain your answer.

Tap Water Is Safe to Drink

Steve Bollard

In the following viewpoint Steve Bollard argues that contrary to popular opinion, most tap water is safe to drink. Because bottled water is not held to the same standards for purity that tap water is, it may even contain more contaminants than heavily filtered and tested tap water. Moreover, plastic particles can seep into bottled water from plastic bottles. Bollard concludes that bottled water is a fashionable trend that does not offer Americans a cleaner source of water than tap water. Bollard is a staff writer for the *Daily Orange,* the independent student newspaper of Syracuse University.

> *"Most Americans are provided with clean, highly refined tap water."*

AS YOU READ, CONSIDER THE FOLLOWING QUESTIONS:
1. What are two waterborne diseases that do not affect many Americans, according to the viewpoint, although they are dangerous to millions of people worldwide?
2. According to the Natural Resources Defense Council, what percentage of Americans drink bottled water?
3. As reported by nutrition professor Sarah Short, how did one-fourth of the bottled water in one study compare with tap water?

Steve Bollard, "Tap Water Misconceptions Fuel Bottled Water Sales," *Daily Orange Online,* April 15, 2004. Reproduced by permission.

Erianne Netherwood-Schwesig tries not to drink tap water. She prefers bottled water because she thinks it's better for her health—even though it costs more.

"It's handy to have (bottled water) right in your room," said Netherwood-Schwesig, a freshman in The College of Arts and Sciences [at Syracuse University]. "It's cleaner, and worth the cost when you buy it in bulk."

With the rising popularity of bottled water, tap water has lost some of its credibility among water connoisseurs. Yet while bottled water

Newly treated water moves through a water treatment facility.

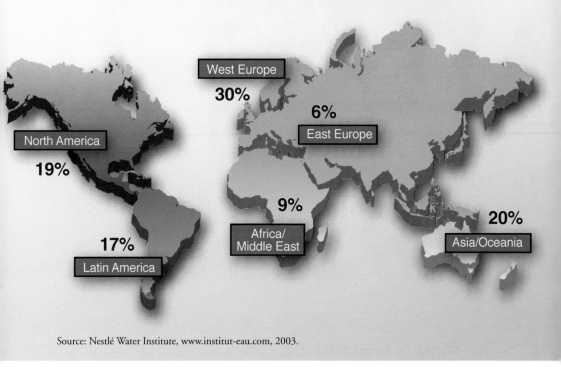

Bottled Water Consumption Worldwide

West Europe
30%

6%
East Europe

North America
19%

9%
Africa/
Middle East

20%
Asia/Oceania

17%
Latin America

Source: Nestlé Water Institute, www.institut-eau.com, 2003.

may be more posh than its tap water counterpart, it may not be as clean—despite the beliefs of those who swear by the bottle.

Some Tap Water Is Contaminated

According to the Natural Resources Defense Council [NRDC], pollution and out-of-date plumbing may be responsible for delivering unhealthy drinking water to residents. In a 2003 report, the NRDC tested the water quality of 19 major cities and found that many cities have deteriorating water sources. Trace elements of arsenic, lead, pesticides and rocket fuel were found in some of these sources.

"Most Americans take it for granted that their tap water is pure and their water infrastructure is safe," said Erik Olson, the report's principal author. "Our report shows that they shouldn't."

Prevalent water-based diseases, such as Guinea worm and schistosomiasis, ravage millions of people each year. Rarely, though, do they infect American tap water drinkers. Instead, most Americans are provided with clean, highly refined tap water.

Like a growing number of Americans, this man's grocery shopping includes stocking up on lots of bottled drinking water.

Tap Water Is Generally Safe

"Generally tap water in the U.S. is quite safe," said Vicki Friedman, spokesperson for Brita Products Company. "When the water leaves the treatment plant, it is in very good shape. When it reaches the municipality, though, it often picks up lead and other sediments through the pipes."

Tony Geiss, deputy director of Onondaga County Water Authority [in New York], said that Syracuse-area tap water goes through a process of coagulation, filtration and disinfection.

"The plant water is very good," he said. "We have very strict criteria to maintain."

Bottled Water Only *Seems* Safer

Bottled water manufacturers have capitalized on the belief that tap water is below consumption standards and use ingenious public relations campaigns to impair the public's view of tap water. In a survey conducted by the American Water Works Association Research Foundation, 35 percent of people surveyed said they drink bottled water because they were worried about the safety of their tap water.

"I like bottled water better," said Adam Krivisky, a freshman acting major. "I watched a '20/20' that said it was cleaner than tap water."

According to an NRDC survey, 54 percent of Americans drink bottled water. Within the last decade, sales of bottled water have tripled, bringing the bottled water industry to a net worth of several billion dollars. The bottled water industry is growing at a rate of eight to 10 percent a year, faster than the rate of any other beverage. There are over 1,000 brands of bottled water, and sales dictate that more are on the way.

This success, however, is surprising given that tap water comes at a much lower cost. It costs 240 to 10,000 times as much to purchase a gallon of bottled water than it does to purchase a gallon of tap water.

Bottled Water May Be Contaminated

The ideal of pure bottled water, however, appears to be nonexistent. In a test conducted by the NRDC, many popular bottled water brands were found to contain levels of contaminants comparable to tap water. Some of the contamination was brought on by the use of plastic bottles, which transfer chemicals to the drinking water.

Aquafina, a division of Pepsi, tested positive for elements of chloroform and other contaminants consistently found in tap water. Other popular brands, such as Poland Spring and Dannon, were also reported to have alien particles in their water.

Bottled water may be perceived as cleaner than tap water, but the standards by which bottled water is graded are much lower. Tap water is tested by the Environmental Protection Agency [EPA], while the Food and Drug Administration [FDA] screens bottled water. While both forms of water are scrutinized, the FDA's tests are not nearly as rigorous as those of the EPA.

> **FAST FACT**
>
> According to the American Water Works Association, more than 94 percent of American water utilities are in full compliance with health-based federal regulations each year.

"Bottled water may not even be as safe as tap water." said Sarah Short, professor of nutrition at Syracuse University. "In one study they found that one-fourth of bottled water had 10 times the bacterial count of tap water."

Even if bottled water violates the standards of the FDA, manufacturers can still offer their product to consumers. They only need label their bottles with warnings of "excessive chemical substances" in the product.

Consumers Make a Choice

Bottled water manufacturers have many opportunities to avoid legislation concerning quality of water, yet innumerable people still opt to purchase their water.

"It's the cool thing to do, lugging bottled water around," Short said. "It's more convenient."

Bottled water drinkers often subject themselves to further dangers by refilling their bottles repeatedly. Some tests indicate that this frequent use of plastic bottles can be unhealthy. A University of Calgary study shows that people who reuse plastic bottles for more than a week—over 88 percent of the population—are risking higher levels of bacteria in their water.

Still, the misconceptions run rampant among those who stick by the bottled water industry.

"I prefer bottled water to the tap water here [in Syracuse]," said Kara Kuncik, sophomore accounting major. "It's just gross. Bottled water tastes better. It's cleaner. I'm really against the water here."

> ### EVALUATING THE AUTHOR'S ARGUMENTS:
>
> This viewpoint and the next viewpoint draw different conclusions about the safety of America's water. Bollard argues that while there are contaminants in some tap water, most Americans are safe. Alan Pell Crawford, on the other hand, argues that America's water is unsafe for consumption. Which argument do you find more persuasive? If you were the head of a family responsible for making choices about the water your family drinks, how would you decide whom to believe? Explain your answer.

Tap Water Is Not Safe to Drink

Alan Pell Crawford

"The scope of the problem of contaminated drinking water is enormous."

In the following viewpoint Alan Pell Crawford examines the problem of groundwater contamination, which he argues makes the water delivered to some homes unsafe to drink. He discusses how tap water can be polluted with cancer-causing chemicals, germs, and poisons such as arsenic. Crawford therefore urges people to drink only bottled or filtered water. Although it is not an ideal solution, he concludes, drinking bottled water can reduce the health risks associated with tap water.

Crawford is a freelance journalist whose articles on history, politics, and public affairs have appeared in the *New York Times, Nation,* and *Vegetarian Times,* where this viewpoint originally appeared.

AS YOU READ, CONSIDER THE FOLLOWING QUESTIONS:

1. In addition to drinking water, in what other ways can people be exposed to polluted water in their daily lives, as described in the viewpoint?

Alan Pell Crawford, "Trouble on Tap: What's Really in Your Water?" *Vegetarian Times,* June 2004, pp. 73–76. Reproduced by permission.

2. What groups of people are especially at risk from polluted water, according to the Natural Resources Defense Council?
3. According to the viewpoint, how many gallons of bottled water does the Mejdrech family go through in one week?

Terry Mejdrech's old home movies just don't afford the same enjoyment they once did. "When I look at those supposedly carefree images of our kids taking baths or laughing while they're splashing in the sprinkler out in the backyard," the 40-year-old Lisle, Illinois, wife and mother says, "I just cringe."

Six years ago, the Illinois Environmental Protection Agency (EPA) informed Mejdrech (pronounced MAY-drek) and 1,500 of her neighbors in this community of large lots and grassy lawns 20 miles west of Chicago that their groundwater had been contaminated by trichloroethylene (TCE), a toxic chemical and carcinogen.

For more than 20 years, starting in the late 1960s, TCE seeped into the neighborhood's aquifer from an industrial plant operated by Lockformer, a company later acquired by Honeywell International Corporation. Honeywell, along with two other companies, agreed in September 2003 to pay $12.5 million in damages, subject to a bankruptcy court's approval. Honeywell and the other defendants in the class-action suit brought by Mejdrech and her neighbors also agreed to pay to hook up the communities to alternative water supplies.

> **FAST FACT**
>
> The average American drank 10.5 gallons of bottled water in 1993, according to the Beverage Marketing Corporation. That figure rose to 22.6 gallons in 2003.

That's cold comfort to the Mejdrechs, who have three boys, 4, 6 and 9 years old, two of whom grew up drinking the contaminated water, taking baths in it, eating food cooked with it off of plates washed in it and wearing clothes laundered in it. "I think about what they did when they were younger and ask myself what effect that exposure might have done to their little bodies," Mejdrech says.

Cause for Concern

In Lisle, a physician whose water supply was also contaminated by TCE from the same plant contracted non-Hodgkin's lymphoma, a form of cancer, and won a $7.2 million settlement. Another resident who drank water allegedly contaminated by TCE from a different plant operating in the same industrial park also contracted non-Hodgkin's lymphoma. A teenager when diagnosed, this young woman is waiting for her day in court, as Mejdrech and her neighbors wait to be added to nearby DuPage County's water supply—or wherever theirs will come from, which has not been decided.

Chris Madden. Reproduced by permission.

"Don't drink that natural spring water
—it's polluted with agrochemicals!"

"The scary thing is, the effect of these chemicals on people's health is supposed to be a long-term thing, so you never know what's in store for you or your kids," Mejdrech explains. "In the meantime, we drink bottled water only, paid for by Honeywell, and the kids take shorter baths, always with the vents on and the bathroom door open. I even wait awhile to let whatever chemicals are in the bath water evaporate, which means colder baths. This is the Chicago area, and it gets cold in winter."

Contaminants in Tap Water

"The scope of the problem of contaminated drinking water is enormous, and the public is just now finding out about decades of environmental misconduct," says Shawn M. Collins of The Collins Law Firm, which has represented the plaintiffs in several of the northern Illinois class-action suits. "In every one of these cases, the government had known there were problems for years before the families found out. You just can't trust the government or business to provide you with safe water or to tell you if your groundwater is contaminated."

The national nonprofit Natural Resources Defense Council (NRDC) announced in June 2003 that a review of reports from the government and from private water suppliers shows that several cities, including Albuquerque, New Mexico, and San Francisco, "have water

A spokesman for the Natural Resources Defense Council announces a 2003 report stating that tap water is threatened by pollution due to old pipes and treatment systems.

This tap water looks clean and clear but may contain germs, lead, arsenic, and even rocket fuel, says a leading environmental group.

that is so contaminated as to pose potential health risks to some consumers, particularly to pregnant women, infants, children, the elderly, and people with compromised immune systems."

Among other substances found in tap water, the NRDC says, are:

- Rocket fuel. A possible carcinogen, perchlorate is in the water of 20 million Americans, with high levels measured in Los Angeles, Phoenix and San Diego.
- Lead. Usually resulting from old pipes, some of them manufactured a century ago, high lead levels have been found in Boston, Newark, Seattle and Washington, DC.
- Germs. Cryptosporidium, an especially troublesome disease-carrying parasite, caused an outbreak of illness in Milwaukee in 1993, sickening 400,000 residents and causing 100 deaths.
- Arsenic. Used in the manufacture of glass, arsenic, "not safe at any level" in drinking water, is present "at significant levels in the drinking water of 22 million Americans," according to the NRDC.

"You can really never know for certain exactly what is in your tap water at any given time, even if your water is treated, because outbreaks do occur," says Kelly A. Reynolds, PhD, an environmental science researcher with the University of Arizona. . . .

Rely on Bottled Water

If, as Collins says, you have no option but to protect yourself, what can you do? The simplest solution is to boil your water. Many consumers, either by choice or—like the Mejdrechs—by necessity, rely on bottled water. Others install home filter systems. There's a range of options for filters that are attached at the tap itself, in price and function, says Reynolds. "Some look for chemicals, others for microorganisms. The one I use is multipurpose, doing both." Home filter systems require maintenance, Lindsay notes. "If you don't change the filter when you are supposed to," she says, "you can actually contribute to the contamination."

What you cannot do is wait for more rigorous federal regulation. Looking out for your own family will require a great deal of adjustment, which Mejdrech says demands more attention than you might expect. "Just reminding yourself—or your kids—not to grab a glass of water any time [you] want it takes some getting used to," she says. "Or [not putting] tap water in the dogs' dish."

Each week, she estimates, the family goes through four 25-gallon jugs of bottled water, the kind installed in office water coolers.

"Bottled water may be good for some things," she says, "but try having to pour water from a jug for boiling pasta. The whole process seems to take forever. Things like that may sound like a little inconvenience, I know, but with everything else we have to contend with now, believe me, they add up."

But if that's as bad as it gets, she'll be thankful.

> **EVALUATING THE AUTHOR'S ARGUMENTS:**
>
> This viewpoint encourages people to use bottled water instead of tap water. The previous viewpoint argued that bottled water is no cleaner than tap water, and may even contain more pollutants. After reading both viewpoints, what is your opinion on bottled water and tap water? Will you drink one over the other? Explain your answer.

Hydrogen Cars Will Reduce Air Pollution

Sophia Cruz

"This colorless, odorless gas is the silver-bullet solution to our transportation, air-pollution, and energy-security concerns."

In the following viewpoint Sophia Cruz argues that hydrogen cars are a solution to many problems—including air pollution—facing the United States. She explains that hydrogen is an abundant and effective energy source that does not produce any of the polluting by-products that gasoline does. Although most of the benefits of hydrogen will not be apparent for more than a decade, she contends, the adaptations that engineers are making to conventional cars today will launch America into the hydrogen age. She concludes that the new cars powered by hydrogen will be appealing to motorists and will emit less pollution.

Cruz is a freelance writer based in Beech Grove, Alabama. She writes frequently for *Associated Content* on subjects including travel, history, and technology.

AS YOU READ, CONSIDER THE FOLLOWING QUESTIONS:
1. What percentage of the country's energy needs will be supplied by hydrogen by the year 2030, if the U.S. Department of Energy's hopes are realized?
2. According to the viewpoint, how much more energy is produced by hydrogen than by gasoline?
3. Why does hydrogen need to be converted to a liquid to be suitable for use as fuel, according to the viewpoint?

Powering your car with water is a fantasy that ranks with turning tin to gold. But the next best thing—H_2O without the O—isn't so farfetched.

[In 2005] California Governor Arnold Schwarzenegger beamed a radiant smile to news cameras while pumping his Hummer's fuel tank full of hydrogen (H_2) at a new Los Angeles International Airport [LAX] station. "What?!" you say. "Isn't that the stuff that blew up the Hindenburg? Is this Terminator W, Revenge of The Public Servants?". . .

[But] hydrogen is back. This time safety measures are available to guard against catastrophe. In fact, prognosticators insist that what's likely to go boom is a global hydrogen economy. In his 2003 State of the Union Address, President [George W.] Bush kicked off a hydrogen initiative with a price tag over $1-billion. The U.S. government's Department of Energy hopes H_2 will handle ten percent of America's energy needs by 2030. A growing number of experts believe this colorless, odorless gas is the silver-bullet solution to our transportation, air-pollution, and energy-security concerns.

> **FAST FACT**
>
> If all U.S. vehicles were switched to hydrogen fuel cell vehicles, some thirty-seven hundred to sixty-four hundred deaths due to pollution each year would be avoided, according to a 2005 Stanford University study.

Highway to the Future

Governor Schwarzenegger seems serious about making hydrogen a star. Calling his specially modified Hummer "a vehicle of today capable of running on the fuel of tomorrow," he's ready to start his SUV's big V-8 and motor on down California's Hydrogen Highway, an initiative aimed at proving the viability of this brave new fuel.

Hydrogen is hot, and not just in California, for two reasons. It's what we'll be pumping into our squeaky/green fuel-cell electric vehicles when they hit the street in 15 or so years. But a growing throng of engineers, scientists and backyard tinkerers are unwilling to wait; this group insists that the engine under the hood of your car can be broken of its gasoline habit and reprogrammed to run just fine on hydrogen. They also contend that lessons learned accumulating, storing, transporting and consuming hydrogen will advance us several miles down the governor's highway to the future.

BMW is hydrogen's biggest corporate booster. In 1978—when fuel cells were still the stuff of space travel—Bavarian engineers began modifying conventional engines to run on H_2. The knowledge they learned will hit the road within five years in the form of production-line 7-series sedans capable of switching between gasoline and hydrogen fuels.

California governor Arnold Schwarzenegger fills up his hydrogen-fueled Hummer at a new station in Los Angeles.

Hydrogen Is Clean and Plentiful

Hydrogen, which consists of one proton and one electron, is nature's most elegant and abundant element. It accounts for three-quarters of the mass and 90-percent of the atoms in the universe. Jupiter is literally full of it. On Earth, hydrogen is the ninth most abundant element, though its tendency to wander off into space makes it a stranger (one part in a million) in our atmosphere.

Combustion experiments began in the 16th century before hydrogen got its name. It burns nicely in air and makes a potent rocket fuel, but hydrogen also has a mean streak (H-bomb).

H_2 is the current darling of internal combustion engine fuels for the same reason it's so attractive for use in electric-car fuel cells: there's no carbon to foul up the energy-conversion process. Burn gas, an amalgamation of hydrogen and carbon, in an engine and most of the by-products spewing out the exhaust contain what's become the evil element (C): carbon monoxide (CO) is what kills you when you lock yourself in the garage

Confidence in the Hydrogen Future

A 2005 poll about future energy needs conducted by the Chevron Corporation asked people the following question: When do you think hydrogen will become a viable part of the solution?

Percentage of Respondents

10 years	25 years	50 years	Never
40%	29%	11%	20%

Source: Chevron Corporation, www.willyoujoinus.com, December 14, 2005.

President George W. Bush speaks about the advantages of hydrogen fuel cell vehicles at a 2006 transportation technology conference in California.

with a car engine running. Partially burned hydrocarbons (HC) are a key constituent of smog. Carbon dioxide (CO_2) is the greenhouse gas under attack for its presumed role in global warming.

Hydrogen, the most potent fuel going, packs nearly three times the energy of gasoline. It's easy to ignite and burns faster and hotter than high-octane gas. The exhaust consists mainly of steam (water in the vapor state). The only carbon by-products come from trace amounts of lubricating oil consumed during combustion. . . .

Hydrogen as Fuel Is Still a Challenge

Were it not for its drawbacks, we'd already be pumping hydrogen into our tanks instead of gasoline. Beyond cost and availability, the major hydrogen headache is that it's a gas at room temperature. Its tiny little atoms slip right through clay, rubber and some metal containers. Condensing it into a liquid state requires cooling it to -423 degrees F, only 37 degrees above absolute zero. In spite of the bother associated with what's called cryogenic (super-cooled) hydrogen, BMW is convinced this is the way to go. . . .

To prove that engines fed hydrogen can be clean AND potent, BMW engineers goaded a 6.0L V-12 [car engine] up to 282 horsepower (without supercharging or turbocharging) and installed it in a special single-seat steamliner dubbed H2R (Hydrogen Record Car). In September, three company drivers circulated a French proving grounds track at speeds over 186 mph [miles per hour]. Nine records were set in a new hydrogen-fueled-vehicle class.

Similar technology will be fitted to a few 7-series sedans that will be offered to retail customers within three to five years, according to BMW. A notable difference is that these cars will be tuned for both hydrogen and gasoline operation to stretch their operating distance. The anticipated driving range is 180 miles on hydrogen and another 375 miles of travel with gasoline.

So the chicken-egg race between hydrogen-powered cars and suitable means of refueling them is heading into the home stretch. The LAX station dedicated by Schwarzenegger . . . is intended for public use within five to ten years. On November 12 [2004], the Clean Energy Pump of Berlin opened for business, ready and able to dispense hydrogen to German motorists. A few hydrogen-powered cars are on the road and more are coming. The age of H_2 transportation has officially begun.

EVALUATING THE AUTHOR'S ARGUMENTS:

This viewpoint you have just read draws some of its power from connecting the idea of hydrogen cars with famous people and products. According to the viewpoint, President George W. Bush and California governor Arnold Schwarzenegger both favor hydrogen-powered cars; and BMW, one of the most prestigious car makers in the world, is working on developing the cars. How does this association with people and products you may have heard about affect whether or not you believe the arguments presented? Explain your answer.

Hydrogen Cars May Not Reduce Air Pollution

Keay Davidson

"Much more research is needed before the nation prematurely commits itself to developing the 'hydrogen economy.'"

In the following viewpoint Keay Davidson outlines some of the challenges that remain before hydrogen fuel cell cars become a reality. Although politicians are hopeful that hydrogen will reduce pollution, Davidson contends that affordable, efficient, and environmentally sound hydrogen cars are still decades away. He explains that the existing technologies for making hydrogen fuel are as polluting as gasoline is now. He concludes that the best hope for reducing pollution with hydrogen cars will come after alternative energies—solar power, wind power, and others—have been developed and expanded.

Davidson is an award-winning science writer for the *San Francisco Chronicle* and for magazines such as *Scientific American* and *New Scientist*.

AS YOU READ, CONSIDER THE FOLLOWING QUESTIONS:

1. What is the richest source of hydrogen today, according to the viewpoint?

Keay Davidson, "Road to Hydrogen Cars May Not Be So Clean; Environmental Peril in Making, Containing Fuel," *San Francisco Chronicle*, December 20, 2004, p. A6. Reproduced by permission of the publisher, conveyed through Copyright Clearance Center, Inc.

2. As Davidson explains, what might be the result of hydrogen escaping into the atmosphere?
3. Why does it matter, according to the viewpoint, how the electricity to make hydrogen is generated?

Auto-industry ads depict hydrogen cars as the vehicular route to clean, blue skies.

President Bush and Gov. Arnold Schwarzenegger are among their biggest champions.

The politicians' enthusiasm for the technology—a leading proposal to solve global warming—is shared by many scientists.

But reality could prove more complex, some critics say. Among the problems detailed at the American Geophysical Union conference in San Francisco [in December 2004]:

- Hydrogen is a very "leaky" gas that could escape from cars and hydrogen plants into the atmosphere. This could set off chemical transformations that generate greenhouse gases that contribute to atmospheric warming.
- The extraction of hydrogen for cars from methane, which is currently the richest available source of hydrogen, will generate carbon dioxide, a major greenhouse gas.
- Hydrogen can also be extracted from ordinary water via a process called electrolysis. However, using current technology, mass electrolysis of water would require intense sources of energy. If those energy sources burn fossil fuels, they, too, would generate greenhouse gases.

These problems are not necessarily showstoppers, and they may be overcome by future technical innovations. In any event, many scientists believe the environmental problems posed by hydrogen cars may prove to be less severe than the problems generated by today's fossil-fuel-dependent cars.

Caution: More Research Is Needed

But given such issues, some experts are cautioning that much more research is needed before the nation prematurely commits itself to developing the "hydrogen economy."

"I'm supportive of research and development, but we are at least two decades away from (deploying) the vehicles on a mass level," said MIT-educated physicist Joseph J. Romm, a former U.S. Department of Energy official, in an interview. Romm's book, *The Hype About Hydrogen: Fact and Fiction in the Race to Save the Climate*, was published [in 2004] by Island Press.

"Americans are very much believers in technology and optimism, and yet when you look at the compelling details" about hydrogen cars, Romm said, "it doesn't make bloody much sense."

Economically, hydrogen devices remain highly unattractive: "Fuel cells are very expensive," Romm said. "The demonstration vehicles all cost hundreds of thousands of dollars." . . .

The Dangers of Leaking Hydrogen

One problem is that hydrogen leaked into the atmosphere binds with oxygen molecules, forming water vapor and clouds. A change in cloud

This hydrogen-fueled car was on display at a California convention in 2006.

abundance in some regions might alter the local temperature and climate—for example, the climate might warm if the clouds trap heat like blankets, or the climate might cool if they reflect sunlight back into space.

"The widespread use of hydrogen fuel cells . . . would cause stratospheric cooling, enhancement of the heterogeneous chemistry that destroys ozone, an increase in noctilucent clouds, and changes in tropospheric (lower-atmosphere) chemistry and atmosphere-biosphere interactions," scientists from Caltech and Jet Propulsion Laboratory

An engineer displays a hydrogen storage vessel he is developing for use in the forthcoming "hydrogen economy."

in Pasadena proposed in the journal *Science* in 2003. Noctilucent clouds are eerie high-altitude clouds whose abundance, some scientists suspect, is influenced by climate change.

Despite the uncertainties about the climatic impact of a hydrogen economy, [University of California–Irvine professor Michael J.] Prather added sardonically, "The promise of a clean, hydrogen-fueled transportation sector has been waved in front of the nation by the current administration, the governor of California and the technologists."

The Risk of Global Warming

And even though optimists say hydrogen will be generated via electrolysis without producing greenhouse gases, the reality is that the oil companies are gearing up to generate it from methane—and the most famous greenhouse gas, carbon dioxide, forms as an unintended byproduct of the methane-treatment process. . . .

Skeptics also point out that because of the hydrogen molecule's small size and volatility, it is an extremely leak-prone gas that must be closely monitored.

Scientists must learn the "potential leak points"—the ways in which hydrogen can leak from cars, plants and other sources—before there is a major shift to a hydrogen economy, Catherine G. Padro of Los Alamos National Laboratory said at the same geophysics session. Scientists, she said, "do not want a repeat of CFCs," or chlorofluorocarbons, the industrial pollutants that started the destruction of part of Earth's atmospheric ozone, which shields us from cancer-causing solar radiation.

But other scientists say that even if hydrogen leakage generates a small amount of global warming, that would be a relatively minor problem compared with the advantages of switching from a fossil-fuel-based transportation system to a system fueled by hydrogen.

> **FAST FACT**
>
> A study conducted by General Motors in 2003 estimates that it would cost $10 billion to set up a series of hydrogen fueling stations within two miles of 70 percent of the U.S. population.

If such a mass switchover to methane-derived hydrogen occurred, the nation's total emission of greenhouse gases could decline between

These wind turbines generate clean electrical power that can be used to create hydrogen for fuel.

10 and 50 percent, according to studies by MIT and Argonne National Laboratory near Chicago, Anthony Eggert, associate director for research in the "Hydrogen Pathways" program at UC [University of California] Davis, said in an interview.

Problems in the Immediate Future

Eggert calls himself a "realistic optimist" about hydrogen cars. On the one hand, he said, "The vehicle itself is not something that you could afford to buy today because the components within the fuel cell system are still very expensive." Also, it wouldn't travel as far on a single "tank" as today's cars: "You'd have to fill up maybe once every 150 to 180 miles."

On the other hand, Eggert said, "The automakers are making incredible progress in reducing costs and increasing reliability and durability."

One problem, skeptics say, is that a switchover to a hydrogen economy may not occur smoothly enough to avoid making environmental troubles in the interim.

"What we cannot do," [geoscientist Kenneth] Deffeyes writes, "is get the electricity (for hydrogen generation) from an existing dirty coal-fired electrical power plant and claim that the environmental bookkeeping begins only after we buy the electricity."

The Long-Term Promise

"If (electrolytic) hydrogen is to be an environmental success, expanding the electrical-generating system necessary to produce it has to be an environmental success," too, he said—which means looking to hydroelectric and geothermal power, as in Iceland, or solar, wind and nuclear power.

The nation's invisible breezes may yet provide a solution.

The United States has enough wind energy—which produces zero greenhouse gases—to electrolytically generate enough hydrogen to support the nation's entire vehicular fleet, said atmospheric scientist Mark Z. Jacobson of Stanford [University] at the geophysics session.

Jacobson showed conference attendees a graphic that pinpointed windy places across the United States—not just in Northern California but also in the Midwest and along the Atlantic coastline—that could support electrolysis for hydrogen-gas fuel plants.

"There's lots of wind out there," he said.

EVALUATING THE AUTHOR'S ARGUMENTS:

Both of the viewpoints you have just read make arguments based primarily on predictions, as the authors describe problems yet to be solved and products yet to be developed. What strategies do the authors use to make their predictions believable? If you find one viewpoint more credible than the other, what leads you to your conclusion?

Facts About Pollution

Editor's note: These facts can be used in reports or papers to reinforce or add credibility when making important points or claims.

Air Pollution
According to the Environmental Protection Agency:
- Driving a car is the single most polluting thing that most Americans do.
- In many cities, cars and trucks are the most significant cause of ground-level ozone pollution.

According to the Sierra Club:
- Cars and light trucks account for 20 percent of the nation's annual carbon dioxide pollution.
- One gallon of gasoline burned puts twenty-eight pounds of carbon dioxide into the atmosphere.

According to a U.S. House of Representatives Committee on Resources Earth Day 2006 announcement:
- Total air emissions have declined 25 percent since 1970.
- Between 1988 and 1997 the number of "unhealthy" air quality days in major U.S. cities decreased an average of 66 percent.
- It now takes twenty new cars to produce the same polluting air emissions as one car produced in the 1960s.

Water Pollution
According to the U.S. House of Representatives Committee on Resources:
- Less than 5 percent of domestic water sources are polluted or severely polluted. In 1961, 30 percent of domestic water sources fell under those categories.
- In 2002 about 94 percent of the population who received their water from community water systems were served by systems meeting all health-based standards. Only 79 percent were served by similarly clean systems in 1993.

- Since the National Coastal Wetlands Conservation Grant Program began in 1990, over 167,000 acres of wetlands have been protected or restored.

According to the Virginia Department of Conservation and Recreation:
- The amount of water on Earth does not change, although it may exist variously as water, ice, or water vapor at different times.
- There are 326 million cubic miles of water on Earth. A cubic mile contains 1.1 trillion gallons.
- Only 3 percent of the Earth's water is freshwater. Two percent is frozen in ice caps and glaciers, leaving only about 1 percent of the Earth's water available for human, plant, and animal consumption.
- Demand for freshwater by humans doubled between 1989 and 2000.
- By 2020 the United States will produce three times the sewage it did in 1970.
- In the Southeast region of the United States, only 8 percent of the stream miles are polluted. Streams in other regions are more polluted: Pacific states, 25 percent; southern plains, 29 percent; northeast, 40 percent; northern plains, 42 percent.

Mercury Pollution
- Forty-five states have issued official warnings that fish in their waters contained levels of mercury high enough to threaten human health.
- The Environmental Protection Agency estimates that half of the mercury in American waterways comes from domestic pollution.
- Mercury pollution has contaminated 10.2 million acres of American lakes, estuaries, and wetlands and 415,000 miles of streams, rivers, and coastline, according to a 2002 estimate by the Environmental Protection Agency.
- Mercury emissions in the United States dropped by more than 42 percent from 1995 to 2006, according to the U.S. House of Representatives Committee on Resources.

Pesticides and Herbicides
According to the World Health Organization:
- Approximately 25 million farmworkers worldwide become sick from pesticide exposure each year.

According to the National Pesticide Telecommunications Network:

- Approximately 90 percent of American families use pesticides at home. They may track additional residues indoors on their shoes, on their hands, or on their pets.
- The amount of pesticide particles in the air is higher inside homes than outside.

The Environmental Protection Agency reports that children are more at risk than adults for exposure to pesticides because

- their bodies are still developing;
- they play on the ground and on the floor more than adults do;
- they put objects into their mouths more than adults do; and
- they consume more pesticide-susceptible foods such as milk, apple juice and applesauce, and orange juice per pound of body weight than adults do.

Recycling

According to the Environmental Protection Agency:

- 42 percent of the paper thrown away in the United States is recycled.
- 40 percent of plastic soft drink bottles are recycled.
- 55 percent of aluminum soft drink and beer cans are recycled.
- 52 percent of major appliances are recycled.

According to the organization Health Care Without Harm:

- With the amount of energy it takes to make one new aluminum can, twenty cans can be made from recycled aluminum.
- One job is created by incinerating 10,000 tons of waste, while dumping the same amount creates 6 jobs and recycling it creates 36 jobs.

According to beverage industry consultant R.W. Beck:

- 40 million plastic bottles—most of them bottled water containers—are thrown in the trash or tossed as litter every day.
- Only 12 percent of plastic bottles from water, juice, and sports beverages are recycled, compared with 30 percent of soft drink bottles.

National Surveys About Pollution

According to a survey released in September 2005 by Hart Associates and Public Opinion Strategies:

- 79 percent of those surveyed were in favor of "stronger national standards" to protect the land, air, and water of the United States, but only 22 percent considered environmental issues as a strong factor in their most recent voting decisions.

According to a Harris poll taken in August 2005:
- 74 percent of people surveyed agreed that "protecting the environment is so important that requirements and standards cannot be too high, and continuing environmental improvements must be made regardless of cost." 24 percent disagreed.
- 47 percent of those surveyed believed that the government's involvement in environmental protection is "too little," while 32 percent believed the government's involvement is "about right" and 19 percent believed the government's involvement is "too much."
- 63 percent of survey participants believed that the general public has done "less than their share" to help solve environmental problems"; 10 percent believed the general public has done "more than their share"; 26 percent believed that the general public's contribution has been "about right."

According to a March 2005 Gallup poll:
- 48 percent of those surveyed believed that the overall quality of the environment in the United States today is "only fair," while 37 percent rated it "good," 10 percent rated it "poor," and 4 percent rated it "excellent."
- 63 percent of people surveyed believed the quality of the environment in the United States is "getting worse," while 29 percent believed that it is "getting better"; 6 percent believed that environmental quality has stayed about the same.

Glossary

aquifer: An underground layer of the earth that holds **groundwater**.

asbestos: A gray fiber made of magnesium silicate. Until the 1970s, asbestos was widely used in clothing, insulation, and other materials to make them fireproof, but then studies showed that exposure to asbestos fibers can cause cancer in humans.

asthma: A disease of the respiratory system that can cause sudden attacks of coughing, chest pressure, and difficulty in breathing.

cap and trade: A policy that regulates the amount of pollutants an industry is allowed to emit. Under cap and trade, individual companies are allowed to emit a specified maximum amount of a pollutant. As an incentive to reduce **emissions**, a company that emits less than its allowance may sell to another company the right to emit the unused part.

carbon dioxide: A gas made of one carbon atom and two oxygen atoms. Carbon dioxide is a by-product of many chemical reactions, including the burning of fossil fuels. Too much carbon dioxide in the atmosphere is believed to cause **global warming**.

carcinogen: A substance that causes cancer.

emissions: Substances that are discharged into the air, especially polluting substances. Polluting emissions come from the chimneys and smokestacks of factories, the tailpipes of cars, and other similar sources.

Environmental Protection Agency (EPA): A federal agency created in 1970 to coordinate the government's efforts to provide and maintain clean air, water, and land. The EPA creates and enforces rules concerning pollution, supports and performs new research, and educates the public about environmental issues.

fine-particle pollution: Air pollution made up of "fine particles," or material 2.5 microns (or 2.5 millionths of a meter, or 0.000098 inch) in diameter or smaller. Because fine particles are so small, they can be inhaled and become embedded in the lungs, where a small amount can do great damage. Also called "small-particle pollution."

global warming: The gradual warming of the earth's atmosphere, caused by human activities including the burning of fossil fuels and **emissions** from industry. Also called "global climate change."

groundwater: Water that exists naturally between layers of soil and rock under the earth's surface. Groundwater is the source of wells and springs.

herbicide: A chemical used to kill plants, especially weeds.

insecticide: A chemical used to kill insects.

methylmercury: A toxic form of mercury that is harmful to the human nervous system.

microbes: Tiny life forms, especially microscopic organisms, including bacteria that cause disease.

neurotoxin: A poisonous substance that damages or destroys nerve tissue.

ozone: A gas molecule made up of three oxygen atoms. High in the atmosphere, it shields the earth from harmful ultraviolet radiation. But at ground level, ozone is a pollutant that can harm the lungs.

pesticide: A chemical used to kill pests, especially insects.

precautionary principle: "Better safe than sorry." The idea that an action that might cause damage should not be taken.

smog: General term for the pollution that is created when chemicals emitted from vehicles combine with each other in the air.

wetlands: Low-lying areas, including swamps, marshes, and fens, that are saturated with water. Wetlands are important filters that remove many impurities from freshwater.

Organizations to Contact

A Better Earth Project
George Mason University, Institute for Humane Studies
3301 N. Fairfax Dr., Suite 440
Arlington, VA 22201
(800) 697-8799
(703) 993-4880
e-mail: info@abetterearth.org
Web site: www.abetterearth.org

A Better Earth is a nonprofit educational organization that promotes innovative thinking about the successes and failures of the environmental movement.

Competitive Enterprise Institute (CEI)
1001 Connecticut Ave. NW, Suite 1250
Washington, DC 20036
(202) 331-1010
e-mail: info@cei.org
Web site: www.cei.org

The Competitive Enterprise Institute, founded in 1984, is a nonprofit public policy organization dedicated to advancing the principles of free enterprise and limited government. CEI argues that the best solutions to environmental problems come from individuals making their own choices in a free marketplace.

Environmental Defense
Membership and Public Information
1875 Connecticut Ave. NW, Suite 600
Washington, DC 20009
(800) 684-3322
e-mail: members@environmentaldefense.org
Web site: www.environmentaldefense.org

Environmental Defense, founded in 1967, works to protect the environmental rights of all people, including future generations, low-income communities, and communities of color. It focuses on U.S. environmental problems and the U.S. role in causing and solving environmental problems.

Greenpeace
702 H St. NW
Washington, DC 20001
(800) 326-0959
e-mail: info@wdc.greenpeace.org
Web site: www.greenpeace.org

Greenpeace is an international nonprofit organization concerned with global threats to the planet's biodiversity and environment.

National Environmental Trust
1200 Eighteenth St. NW, 5th Fl.
Washington, DC 20036
(202) 887-8800
e-mail: info@net.org
Web site: www.net.org

The National Environmental Trust is a nonprofit, nonpartisan organization established in 1994 to inform citizens about environmental problems and how they affect human health and quality of life. Its educational programs focus on clean air, global warming, energy, and other environmental issues.

National Recycling Coalition
1325 G St. NW, Suite 1025
Washington, DC 20005
(202) 347-0450
Web site: www.nrc-recycle.org

The National Recycling Coalition is a nonprofit organization dedicated to the advancement and improvement of recycling, source reduction, composting, and reuse.

Natural Resources Defense Council (NRDC)
40 W. Twentieth St.
New York, NY 10011
(212) 727-2700

e-mail: nrdcinfo@nrdc.org
Web site: www.nrdc.org

NRDC is an environmental action organization that supports pro-environmental legislation. It calls on government to work with its citizens to reduce pollution, protect endangered species, and create a sustainable way of life for humankind.

Sierra Club
85 Second St., 2nd Fl.
San Francisco, CA 94105
(415) 977-5500
e-mail: information@sierraclub.org
Web site: www.sierraclub.org

Founded in 1892, the Sierra Club is the oldest and largest grassroots environmental organization in the United States. Its mission is to help people explore, enjoy, and protect the wild places of the earth and practice and promote the responsible use of the earth's ecosystems and resources.

Union of Concerned Scientists
2 Brattle Square
Cambridge, MA 02238-9105
(617) 547-5552
Web site: www.ucsusa.org

The Union of Concerned Scientists is an independent nonprofit alliance of citizens and scientists concerned about the misuse of science and technology in society. It sponsors the Sound Science Initiative, through which scientists provide information on environmental science to government and the media.

U.S. Fuel Cell Council
1100 H St. NW, Suite 800
Washington, DC 20005
(202) 293-5500
Web site: www.usfcc.com

The council is an industry association dedicated to making fuel cells commercially available in the United States. Its members include the world's leading fuel cell developers, manufacturers, suppliers, and customers.

Worldwatch Institute
1776 Massachusetts Ave. NW
Washington, DC 20036-1904
(202) 452-1999
e-mail: worldwatch@worldwatch.org
Web site: www.worldwatch.org

Worldwatch Institute is a research institution that analyzes and focuses attention on global problems, including environmental issues such as pollution and the relationship between trade and the environment.

For Further Reading

Books

Blatt, Harvey, *America's Environmental Report Card: Are We Making the Grade?* Cambridge, MA: MIT Press, 2005. This readable analysis of the current state of the environment in the United States is well supported with statistics, charts, and illustrations.

Brummet, Dave, and Lillian Brummet, *Trash Talk: An Inspirational Guide to Saving Time and Money Through Better Waste and Resource Management.* Baltimore: PublishAmerica, 2004. A lighthearted and optimistic collection of simple ideas anyone can use to reduce, reuse, and recycle.

Burnie, David, *Endangered Planet.* Boston: Kingfisher, 2004. Directed at middle-school readers, this book describes the current state of various ecosystems, and explains measures, including recycling, that can be taken to slow humankind's harmful effects.

Clark, Tony, *Inside the Bottle: An Exposé of the Bottled Water Industry.* Ottawa, ON: Polaris Institute, 2005. Written with the general consumer in mind, this book explains where bottled water comes from, how it is marketed, and what happens to the empty bottles. Clark argues that although bottled water is necessary in emergencies and in remote areas, most bottled water purchases are a waste of money and resources.

Cone, Marla, *Silent Snow: The Slow Poisoning of the Arctic.* New York: Grove, 2005. Environmental journalist Cone traces the path of industrial toxins carried by wind and water to the people of the Arctic, whose bodies contain high levels of contaminants.

Davis, Devra, *When Smoke Ran Like Water: Tales of Environmental Deception and the Battle Against Pollution.* New York: Basic, 2002. Considers the consequences of industrial pollution.

DuPuis, E. Melanie, *Smoke and Mirrors: The Politics and Culture of Air Pollution.* New York: New York University Press, 2004. Examines air pollution policy through the twin lenses of science and social justice.

Exum, Kaitlen Jay, and Lynn Messina, eds., *The Car and Its Future.* New York: H.W. Wilson, 2004. An anthology including five articles on alternative vehicles and fuels.

Fujita, Rodney M., *Heal the Ocean: Solutions for Saving Our Seas.* Gabriola Island, BC: New Society, 2003. Written by a marine ecologist, this book presents stories of successful efforts to restore polluted waterways, and offers suggestions for new projects.

Gallant, Roy A., *Atmosphere: Sea of Air.* New York: Benchmark, 2003. Science writer Gallant gives an overview of how the atmosphere was formed and how it functions, explains current threats from pollution, and offers possible solutions. Geared for middle-school readers, this book contains excellent maps, charts, and photographs.

Huber, Peter W., *Hard Green: Saving the Environment from the Environmentalists—Conservative Manifesto.* New York: Basic, 2000. An engineer and attorney, Huber examines environmentalists' efforts from a free-market perspective, concluding, for example, that recycling is a wasted effort. He argues that creative thinking and the marketplace will solve pollution issues.

Kimbrell, Andrew, ed., *The Fatal Harvest Reader: The Tragedy of Industrial Agriculture.* Washington, DC: Island, 2002. A collection of essays contending that industrial agriculture as it is generally practiced is harmful to the land, air, and water. Argues for more organic and sustainable food production.

Lomborg, Bjorn, *The Skeptical Environmentalist.* Cambridge, England: Cambridge University Press, 2002. Statistician Lomborg analyzes various claims made by environmentalists, concluding that some are correct, some are exaggerated, and some are still poorly understood.

Markowitz, Gerald, and David Rosner, *Deceit and Denial: The Deadly Politics of Industrial Pollution.* Berkeley and Los Angeles: University of California Press, 2002. A well-researched historical account of the conflict between the public's demand for new products and the demand for a cleaner environment.

McDaniel, Carl N., *Wisdom for a Livable Planet.* San Antonio: Trinity University Press, 2005. Profiles of eight men and women who have dedicated their lives to solving environmental problems including hazardous waste, climate change, and the overuse of polluting chemicals in agriculture.

McDonough, William, and Michael Braungart, *Cradle to Cradle: Remaking the Way We Make Things.* New York: North Point, 2002. An architect and a chemist call for "eco-effectiveness," or new ways to make products without generating waste that will eventually need to be recycled.

Milloy, Steven J., *Junk Science Judo: Self-Defense Against Health Scares and Scams.* Washington, DC: Cato Institute, 2001. A lively analysis debunking many perceived environmental health threats and warnings about food.

Romm, Joseph J., *The Hype About Hydrogen: Fact and Fiction in the Race to Save the Climate.* Rev. ed. Washington, DC: Island, 2005. Written by a former staff member of the U.S. Department of Energy, this book provides an overview of the technology of hydrogen fuel cells. It argues against devoting national funds and attention to a hydrogen fuel cell future.

Ropeik, David, and George Gray, *Risk: A Practical Guide for Deciding What's Really Safe and What's Dangerous in the World Around You.* Boston: Houghton Mifflin, 2002. This volume analyzes the dangers posed by pollutants, cell phones, and other perceived threats, and suggests ways consumers can make safe and simple choices.

Royte, Elizabeth, *Garbage Land: On the Secret Trail of Trash.* Boston: Little, Brown, 2005. Curious about where her discarded Fig Newtons ended up, Elizabeth Royte investigated what happens to Americans' household garbage after it is thrown away. A highly readable book.

Schwartz, Joel, *No Way Back: Why Air Pollution Will Continue to Decline.* Washington, DC: AEI, 2003. Argues that the United States will continue to significantly reduce air pollution. More fuel-efficient cars and cleaner power plants will make air cleaner, not more polluted, in the future.

Vigil, Kenneth M., *Clean Water: An Introduction to Water Quality and Pollution Control.* Corvallis: Oregon State University Press, 2003. This well-illustrated guide to the scientific and political issues of safe water is written in clear, nontechnical language for general readers.

Periodicals

Benevento, Douglas H., "Facing Up to Future Smog: Controlling Pollution More Difficult than 30 Years Ago," *Denver Post,* June 20, 2004.

Bernstein, Mark, and David Whitman, "Smog Alert: The Challenges of Battling Ozone Pollution," *Environment,* October 2005.

Christopher, Tom, "Turf Wars," *House and Garden,* August 2004.

Cottle, Michelle, "Earth Mothers on Patrol," *Time,* April 18, 2005.

Easterbrook, Gregg, "Clear Skies, No Lies," *New York Times,* February 16, 2005.

Eastland, Juliet, "I'm Recycling as Fast as I Can," *Orion Online,* October 2005. www.oriononline.org.

Ebersole, René, "Is Your Drinking Water Safe?" *National Wildlife,* June/July 2004.

Fink, David, "Making Mercury Matters Worse," *National Wildlife,* April/May 2004.

Fumento, Michael, "Cleaner Air Brings Dirtier Tricks," *Tech Central Station,* July 9, 2004. www.techcentralstation.com.

Gubeno, Jackie, "New Kid in Town: The Emergence of Hybrid-Fueled Cars Could Boost the Number of Nickel-Metal Hydride Batteries in the Recycling Stream," *Recycling Today,* January 2005.

Harder, B., "Particles' Harm Varies by Person, Region, Season," *Science News,* March 26, 2005.

Kester, Corinna, "Diesels Versus Hybrids: Comparing the Environmental Costs," *World Watch,* July/August 2005.

Knopper, Melissa, "Clearing the Air," *E: The Environmental Magazine,* July/August 2005.

Kuzemchak, Sally, "Should You Buy Organic?" *Parents,* April 2005.

Lieberman, Ben, "New York Summer Without New York Smog?" *New York Post,* September 15, 2004.

Loecher, Barbara, "Is Your Water Fit to Drink?" *Prevention,* April 2004.

Long, Chery, "Hazards of the World's Most Common Herbicide," *Mother Earth News,* October/November 2005.

Lumiere, Erica, "Fish: Healthy or Toxic?" *Harper's Bazaar,* May 2004.

Magnarelli, Margaret, and Peter Jaret, "Is Your Family's Water Safe?" *Good Housekeeping,* February 2005.

Markels, Alex, and Randy Dotinga, "Don't Go in the Water," *U.S. News & World Report,* August 16, 2004.

Milius, Susan, "Foraging Seabirds Carry Contaminants Home," *Science News,* July 16, 2005.

Milloy, Steven, "Pesticides Not a Threat to Students," *Fox News.com,* August 9, 2005. www.foxnews.com.

Mother Jones, "The Asthma Trap," March/April 2005.

Naughton, Keith, "Hybrid Nation? Nope," *Newsweek,* October 10, 2005.

Rio, Robert, "Mercury: Grain of Truth, Gram of Nonsense," *Heartland Institute,* March 1, 2004. www.heartland.org.

Roth, Zachary, "Monster Truck Rally: Defending the SUV," *Washington Monthly,* December 2003.

Shermer, Michael, "Bottled Twaddle: Is Bottled Water Tapped Out?" *Scientific American,* July 2003.

Simmons, Andy, and Richard Sacks, "Clean Machines," *Reader's Digest,* April 2004.

Truett, Richard, "Automakers Think Green," *Automotive News,* November 1, 2004.

Wooten, Jim, "Ignore Gloom: Environment Will Survive," *Atlanta Journal-Constitution,* April 19, 2005.

Zuniga, Daphne, "Tuna on Rye—Hold the Mercury, Please," *O, the Oprah Magazine,* April 2005.

Web Sites

Cato Institute: Environment and Climate (www.cato.org/research/nat-studies/index.html). The Cato Institute is a libertarian think tank that seeks to protect the environment without unnecessary government intervention. Includes a reading list with articles promoting libertarian, free-market approaches to environmental protection and skepticism about environmentalist claims.

The Commons: Environmental Alarmism Archives (http://commonsblog.org/archives/cat_environmental_alarmism.php). A collection of blog postings analyzing the harmful effects of exaggerating the seriousness of environmental problems; topics include air quality, pollution, recycling, water, and more. Includes a free-market environmentalism reading list with links to many articles online.

Environmental Protection Agency (www.epa.gov). The Environmental Protection Agency (EPA) is a government agency that works to develop and enforce environmental laws enacted by Congress.

Grist Magazine (www.grist.org). An online magazine featuring independent environmental news and commentary, with the slogan "doom and gloom with a sense of humor." Offers a free e-mail newsletter.

Truthout Environment (http://truthout.org/environment.shtml). A reader-supported site that provides links to recent news stories and opinion pieces on environmental issues, including ways the U.S. government and large corporations contribute to pollution and global warming. Offers a free e-mail subscription.

Index

Solid Waste Association of North America, 94
Solomon, Gina, 42
State of the Air (American Lung Association), 15
Susquehanna River, 28
Szwarc, Sandy, 63

Talent, Jim, 92
Thompson, Mike, 92
Townsend, Timothy, 94
Trasande, Leo, 57–58
trichloroethylene, 104–105
2,4-D (herbicide), 73–75

volatile organic compounds, 19–20

Walke, John, 58

Wall Street Journal (newspaper), 66
wastewater treatment plants, 31, 33, 37
water, 35–36
  bottled, 99, 104
    contamination of, 101–102
  ground, 104–105
  tap, 99–101
    contamination of, 106–107
water pollution, 30, 36–38
West Nile virus, 82
wetlands, losses of, 31–32, 37, 38
Whitman, Christine Todd, 33
Wilson, Matthew, 71, 72, 76
Wodder, Rebecca R., 27
Wyden, Ron, 92, 93

Picture Credits

Cover: Christopher Furlong/Getty Images
Maury Aaseng, 23, 30, 66, 87, 99, 112
Mario Anzuoni/Reuters/Landov, 117
AP/Wide World Photos, 10, 18, 24, 26, 29, 32, 36, 39, 44, 53, 54, 61, 68, 72, 79, 83, 92, 95, 100, 106, 111, 118
Frederic J. Brown/AFP/Getty Images, 16
© China Newsphoto/Reuters/CORBIS, 14
Mike Clarke/AFP/Getty Images, 41
Tim Graham/Getty Images, 107
© Robert Landau/CORBIS, 11
Erik S. Lesser/Getty Images, 47
Darren McCollester/Getty Images, 80
© Will & Deni McIntyre/CORBIS, 60
Newhouse News Service/Landov, 75
Mandel Ngan/AFP/Getty Images, 113
Photos.com, 12, 120
© Mark Richards/CORBIS, 51
© Charles E. Rotkin/CORBIS, 35
© Bob Sacha/CORBIS, 86
Brian Snyder/Reuters/Landov, 65
Donald Stout/Newhouse News Service/Landov, 93
Mario Tama/Getty Images, 46
© Alan Towse; Ecoscene/CORBIS, 98

About the Editor

Cynthia A. Bily teaches writing and literature at Adrian College in Adrian, Michigan. She has written hundreds of nonfiction pieces for reference books and other educational publications. Her most recent book for Greenhaven Press was *Opposing Viewpoints: Global Warming*. She lives in Adrian with her husband, son, and two cats.